Challenge and Change:
History of the Jews in America

Early Settlement Through
Central European Migration

Written by: Shelley Kapnek Rosenberg, Ed.D.

Historian and Researcher: Alice L. George, Ph.D.

Historian: Reena Sigman Friedman, Ph.D.

Historical Consultant: Jonathan D. Sarna, Ph.D.

Educational Consultants, Auerbach Central Agency for Jewish Education:
Nancy M. Messinger, Rochelle Buller Rabeeya, and Helene Z. Tigay

Project Directors:
Nancy Isserman
Murray Friedman

BEHRMAN HOUSE, INC.

Designer: Julia Prymak, Pryme Design

Project Editor: Terry Kaye, Behrman House, Inc.

Front Cover Images:
From standing figure and continuing clockwise: Uriah P. Levy, Abigail Franks, Adolph Frankel, Sam Frankel, Haym Salomon, George Washington, Robert Morris, Rebbeca Gratz, and Isaac Mayer Wise.

Credits:
Deputation of Jews Before Ferdinand and Isabella, courtesy of Picture Collection, The Branch Libraries, The New York Public Library, Astor, Lenox, and Tilden Foundation (contents page, p. 4 and back cover)

Exterior of Touro Synagogue, courtesy of John T. Hopf (p. 7)

Maps of colonization by William R. Sheppard, C.S. Hammond & Company, 1929 (p. 9)

Map of Jewish communities in the colonies, adapted from *Jews and the Founding of the Republic,* edited by Jonathan Sarna, Beeny Kraut, and Samuel K. Joseph (New York: Markus Weiner Publishing, 1985). Copyright Hebrew Union College–Jewish Institute of Religion. With permission of Jonathan D. Sarna, and Hebrew Union College–Jewish Institute of Religion (p. 15)

Haym Salomon stamp, courtesy of the U.S. Postal Service (contents page and p. 29)

Portrait of *Judah Touro,* courtesy of Redwood Library and Athenaeum, Newport, Rhode Island (p. 41)

Portrait of *Rebecca Gratz* by Thomas Sully, courtesy of Rosenbach Museum and Library, Philadelphia (front cover, title page, and p. 46)

Map of Europe 1815, Longmans, Green, and Co., 1914 (p. 51)

First Jewish immigrants to enter Galveston, Texas, in 1907, courtesy of the UT Institute of Texas Cultures at San Antonio, no. 73-938 (p. 59)

Map of the United States since 1855 by William R. Sheppard, C.S. Hammond & Company, 1929 (p. 61)

Chrome postcard entitled "Levi Strauss Copper Riveted Overalls, Levi's Electric Rodeo—The Talk of Treasure Island," from the Golden Gate International Exposition, 1939, The Autry Museum of Western Heritage, Los Angeles, donated by Ms. Nancy S. Jackson (contents page and p. 64)

Galveston immigrant and his predecessor (Adolph and Sam Frankel in Cushing, Oklahoma), from Allen Mondell and Cynthia Salzman Mondell's film *West of Hester Street* (front cover, title page, and p. 68)

Hominy cowboy, courtesy of the Collection of Daniel Katz (p. 69 and back cover)

All other photographs, courtesy of American Jewish Historical Society, Newton Center, Massachusetts and New York, New York.

This textbook has been funded by Righteous Persons Foundation, The Farber Foundation, and private donors.

Copyright © 2004 by Behrman House, Inc.
Springfield, New Jersey
www.behrmanhouse.com

ISBN: 0-87441-197-1
Manufactured in the United States of America

Contents

Unit 1:
Jews in the New World

Unit 2:
The Revolutionary War
and the New Republic

Unit 3:
Central European Jews Come to America

What effect did prejudice and intolerance have on Jews in the Old and New Worlds?

You probably know the famous rhyme "In fourteen hundred and ninety-two, Columbus sailed the ocean blue." But did you know that right around the time King Ferdinand gave Columbus permission for his trip, he expelled all the Jews from Spain? The king confiscated their property and possessions and sold them, using the money to help pay for Columbus's second voyage to the New World a year later. What led up to this cataclysmic event?

THE DILEMMA BEGINS

In the early eighth century, Muslim invaders conquered Spain from its Christian rulers. Jews had been persecuted in Spain prior to the Muslim conquests. Under Muslim rule, however, Spain became a favorable place for Jews to settle. Jews from North Africa and other places immigrated to the area and for centuries participated in the political, economic, and cultural life of Muslim Spain.

Even after the Muslim conquests, small Christian kingdoms had remained in the north of Spain. Over a period of several hundred years, the Christians reconquered Spain. Although Jews initially fared well under Christian rulers, anti-Jewish feeling increased, and in 1391, riots broke out in which many Jews were killed. Many converted to Christianity to save their lives. They were called Conversos and were forbidden by church law ever to practice Judaism again. Even so, many of them kept their faith and tried to practice Judaism in secret. These people were often called Marranos. This is a derogatory term, probably from the Spanish word for "swine."

In 1233 CE, the Catholic Church had begun the Holy Inquisition to find and punish people the Church considered **heretics.**

CE stands for "common era." This term is used by Jews to refer to the time after the birth of Jesus. Other people call this period AD or "anno Domini," which means "in the year of Our Lord." Jews refer to events that happened before the birth of Jesus as BCE, which means "before the common era." Other people call this time BC, or "before Christ."

Christians who hold religious opinions that are different from the generally accepted beliefs may be considered **heretics** by those in the majority.

A delegation of Spanish Jews appears before Ferdinand and Isabella, beseeching the monarchs to repeal their expulsion edict. Torquemada, the grand inquisitor, at right, urges otherwise.

Then, in 1481, King Ferdinand and Queen Isabella of Spain got permission from the pope to begin their own inquisition in Spain. They wanted to find Jews who supposedly had converted to Christianity but really had not. They feared that these secret Jews would "Judaize" the other Conversos who had not returned to Judaism. The Spanish Inquisition tortured people to make them confess to being unfaithful to the church. Finally, on a fateful day in 1492, the Jews were expelled from Spain. The Spanish government saw their expulsion as the only way to keep them from influencing Jews who had converted to Christianity.

What do you think the word Judaize means?

GIVING PORTUGAL AND HOLLAND A TRY

Many Jews fled to Portugal for safety, but Portugal did not remain a safe haven for long. In 1497, there was a marriage between the Spanish and Portuguese royal families, and the Jews again faced expulsion. However, the Portuguese government did not want to lose the Jews' wealth. Therefore, many Portuguese Jews were forced to take part in group baptisms and were not allowed to leave the country. Such conversions strengthened their commitment to the Conversos. Many Jews started to practice their religion in secret again. Some managed to escape, however, and went to other parts of Europe and to North Africa, as well as to the Spanish and Portuguese colonies in the New World. But the Inquisition followed, and in 1518, Converso settlements in the Americas were forbidden.

Some Jews who left Portugal found safety in the Netherlands. They were **Sephardic** Jews, who used Spanish and Portuguese in their religious services and followed many distinctive rituals and traditions. They were used to interacting with non-Jews and were somewhat open to secular—nonreligious—learning. By 1581, Holland had won its independence from Spain. The Dutch, who were **Calvinist,** accepted other religions and strongly opposed the Inquisition. The country was also a major center for trade. It seemed to be the perfect place for people searching for a new life.

The Spanish and Portuguese Jews—known as **Sephardic** Jews, from the Hebrew word for "Spain"—came to the New World searching for freedom from religious persecution. They were the first to create Jewish communities in the New World.

A **Calvinist** is a Protestant who follows the teachings of the theologian John Calvin.

BRIEF SUCCESS . . . AND THEN DISAPPOINTMENT

Conditions got even better for the Jews—who wanted their own community—after the Dutch captured Pernambuco, Brazil, in 1630. The Dutch West India Company governed the colony and wanted it to be a success. The company recruited Jewish settlers and gave them the same rights as those given to Christians—something unheard of before. For example, no one could legally take possession of their homes or force them to convert. Since many Jews already spoke Portuguese (the language of Brazil), the colony became a popular destination for Jewish refugees. By the 1640s, there were more than 1,000 Jews there, about one-third of the colony's white population.

Most of the Jews settled in and around the city of Recife. Two synagogues were established, and Recife became the first legally recognized Jewish community in the New World. There were rabbis from Europe and two Jewish schools. Still, there was a threat that the Portuguese might recapture the colony. To persuade the Jews to stay, the Dutch West India Company offered them complete equality as members of the colony.

Unfortunately, the freedom the Jews found in Recife lasted only a short time. In 1654, the Portuguese recaptured the colony. By then, only 600 Jews were left, and again they were expelled. Some returned to Holland while others searched for a new place to live in the New World.

What would you have done at this point?

ON TO NEW AMSTERDAM

On February 24, 1654, some of the Recife refugees set sail, expecting to land on the Caribbean island of Martinique, but their ship was captured by a Spanish **privateer** and forced to sail to Jamaica, which was under Spanish control. There, the Jews' few possessions, except for their clothing and furniture, were confiscated. The leaders of the Inquisition had several of the baptized Jews imprisoned. The rest—about twenty-three mainly Dutch and Italian Jews—were allowed to leave with the other passengers. They landed in Cuba and quickly made arrangements to sail on a ship named the *Saint Catherine.* They headed for New Amsterdam, a settlement on the western side of what we now call Manhattan, which was part of the Dutch colony of New Netherland.

The situation in New Amsterdam was not what the Jews had hoped for. The few Jews already there were **Ashkenazic** traders from Central Europe who were simply passing through. Upon their arrival, the refugees were stripped of their possessions because they could not pay the full cost of their passage. The ship's captain won a court order to auction off their furniture. When that failed to raise enough money, two Jews were imprisoned in the stockade. Others lived off handouts from the Ashkenazic traders.

It is a wonder that this small band of Jews, who braved such odds to come to the New World, survived at all. But they did survive.

A **privateer** is a privately owned warship hired by a government to fight enemy ships.

Jews from Central and Eastern Europe—called **Ashkenazic** Jews, from the Hebrew word for "Germany"—first came to America as traders. They, too, were happy to find religious freedom, and eventually they outnumbered the Sephardic Jews.

How were the Jews like the Pilgrims?

The Jews who arrived in New Amsterdam from Recife in 1654 and established the first Jewish community in North America have been compared to the Pilgrims who landed on Plymouth Rock in 1620. Both groups wanted freedom to worship in whatever way they chose, but the Pilgrims came by choice and had some money. Most of the Jews who came to the New World had been expelled from their homes, and all of their possessions and money had been confiscated. The Pilgrims wanted a colony of their own; the Jews wanted to live among the other colonists in New Amsterdam. We can see that although these two groups were similar in one critical way, they also had important differences.

FINALLY . . . A HOME

The British took control of New Amsterdam in 1664 and changed its name to New York. Jews continued to immigrate to the New World, and in the year 1700, there were about 250 Jews out of a total population of 250,000 settlers and slaves in the British colonies in North America.

The Jewish community has always been a minority in the United States. What makes you aware of that today?

After the British won the French and Indian War and new territory was opened to settlement, some Jews chose to move west. Most, however, remained in East Coast port cities. Jews established communities in Savannah, Georgia (in 1733); Newport, Rhode Island, and Charleston, South Carolina (in the 1750s); and Philadelphia (in the 1760s). Each of these settlements offered religious freedom and a chance to make a decent living. Colonial Jews held a wide variety of jobs. By 1776, New York had the largest number of Jews of any city in North America—about 350.

The community in Savannah did not survive long. War had broken out between Spain and England. In 1740, fearing an invasion by Spain, all but three Jewish families left. The community did not begin holding prayer services again, in private homes, until 1774. They still followed Sephardic traditions even though, by then, the lay leaders were Ashkenazic.

In Charleston and Philadelphia, Jews met only privately until the Revolutionary War. The Newport Jewish community, with the financial support of the New York Jewish community, built a synagogue, which was consecrated in 1763. Now known as Touro Synagogue, it is the oldest synagogue in the United States. It was named, in the nineteenth century, in memory of Isaac Touro, the congregation's first *hazan.*

By the end of the eighteenth century, there were between 2,000 and 2,500 Jews living in the United States. The "wandering Jews" had finally found a home.

What do you think it would take to make you leave your home and travel around the world to seek your fortune in a strange new land? Would you do it to support your family? Would you do it to practice your religion in peace? Can you think of other times when Jews in other countries had to make the same difficult decision?

What's in a name?

Religion was one important factor motivating the Jews who came to the New World. Many believed that the movement of Jews all over the world was a sign of the time when the Messiah would come. They gave their synagogues Hebrew names that demonstrated this hope, as well as hope for a new life in America: Mikveh Israel (Hope of Israel) in Philadelphia, Pennsylvania; Shearith Israel (Remnant of Israel) in New York, New York; and Jeshuat Israel (Salvation of Israel) in Newport, Rhode Island.

Newport's famed Touro Synagogue.

DO IT

Find out about the Hebrew names of synagogues. What is the name of your synagogue? of other synagogues in your community? What do the names mean? What do they tell you about the hopes, dreams, and expectations of the people who founded them?

From mother to son

The following excerpt is from a letter from Abigail Franks, dated July 9, 1733, to her son Naphtali Franks, "To be left att Tom's Coffe House & behinde the Royall Exchange In London." The Franks were well-known members of New York society. Abigail's many letters have historical significance because they were among the first letters written by a Jewish woman in New York. They give us a special look into the life of the people at the time.

THINK ABOUT IT
What was Abigail's advice to her son? Why might she have chosen to write what she did? Put yourself in Abigail's place. If you lived at that time, what would you write to your son or daughter?

Dear HertSey . . .

I have Soe Offten recommended You to be Wary in y[ou]r conduct that I will not Again make a Repetition but this I must recom[men]d to you not to be Soe free in y[ou]r Discourse on religeon and be more circumspect in the Observence of some things Especialy y[ou]r morning Dev[otio]ns for tho' a Person may think freely and Judge for themselves they ought not to be to free of Speach nor to make a Jest of wath ye multitude in A Society think is of the Last Consequence and As You Observed to me some time agoe you wondered Any one Could Take amiss if his Neighbour did not goe the Same Road. pray why are You Soe Intent by your Disputes to think Anyone will follow you It Shows in one of your Age a Self-Opinion wich Quality I would have you Carfuly avoid for it will grow opon you with time if not Nipt in the bud. You wrote me Some time agoe you was asked at my brother Ashers to a fish Dinner but you did not Goe I Desire you will Never Eat Anything with him Unless it be bread & butter nor noe where Else where there is the Least doubt of things not done after our Strict Judaicall method for wathever my thoughts may be Concerning Some Fables this and Some other foundementalls I Look Opon the Observence Conscientioussly and therefore with my blessing I Strictly injoyn it to your care . . .
your Loveing mother,
Abigail Franks

CHAPTER 2

BATTLING FOR RIGHTS

The twenty-three Jews who boarded a ship in Recife, Brazil, heading for New Amsterdam had high hopes. They were looking forward to a new and better life. Remember, Jews had fled the Inquisition, first in Spain and then in Portugal, and had become Dutch subjects. They had tried their luck in Recife and had enjoyed a certain amount of freedom there. While Holland had a state religion, Calvinism, in Recife the official policies were toned down, both by the Dutch people's openness to other religions and by practical concerns—the Dutch wanted the colony to be a success. Then the Portuguese recaptured the colony, and Jews were forced to flee yet again.

CHALLENGES FROM THE START

In New Amsterdam, it was a different story. The colony's leader, Governor Peter Stuyvesant, a member of the Dutch Reformed Church, did not want Jews to settle in his colony. He made his position clear. He rejected them because of their religion and said that he considered them untrustworthy as well. He wrote a letter to the directors of the Dutch West India Company in Holland, who controlled the colony, saying that "the deceitful race—such hateful enemies and **blasphemers** of the name of Christ—be not allowed to further infect and trouble this new colony."

Blasphemers are people who speak about God without respect.

The Jews of New Amsterdam challenged Stuyvesant. They wrote to the leaders of the Portuguese Jewish community in Holland and asked for help. These men were important merchants in Amsterdam. They wrote to the directors of the company on behalf of the Jews in the New World, asking that the newly arrived colonists be given permission to remain in New Amsterdam with all of the same rights that they would have enjoyed at home in Holland. Stuyvesant received orders that the Jews be permitted to join the colony as long as the Jewish poor did not become a burden to the community.

THE BEGINNING OF PROGRESS

Life was not easy for the settlers. Though at first they faced many restrictions, within three years they had won the right to own land, conduct trade, and hold private worship services. These are all rights we now take for granted, but at that time there was still debate over whether Jews could become citizens, vote, hold public office, testify as witnesses in court, hire Christian servants, or be excused from the special laws that made Sunday a day of rest. In fact, such issues arose wherever Jews lived in the New World.

Why were these rights so important to the Jewish colonists? Why might the Christian majority have wanted to deny Jews these rights? What rights do you have in America today that are especially important to you?

The Jews persisted—and made progress. In 1655, three Jews requested the right to purchase land for the first Jewish cemetery. Stuyvesant granted them "a little hook of

The Journey to the New World

Trace the Jews' wanderings from the Inquisition in Spain through their arrival in the New World. Circle the following places:

Spain   Recife (Pernambuco), Brazil

Portugal   Jamaica

The Netherlands   New Amsterdam

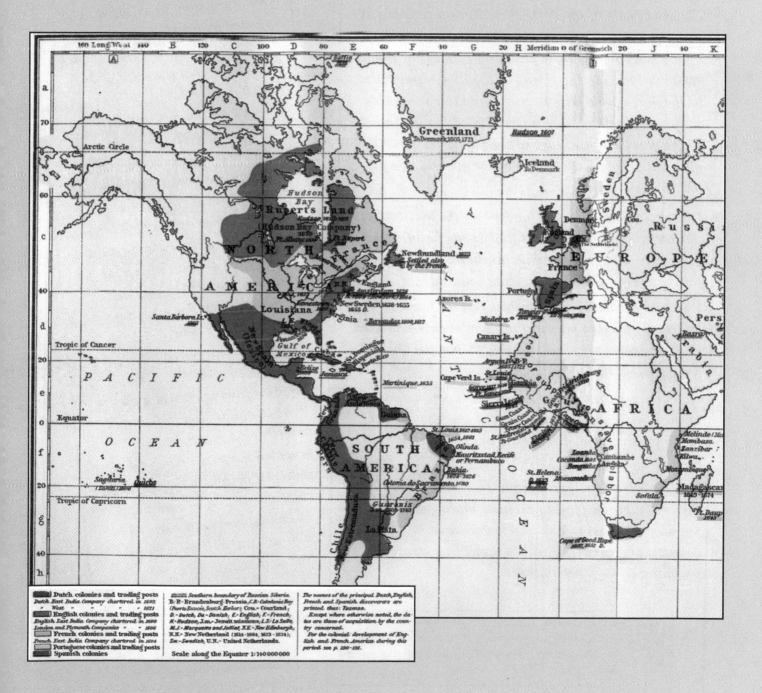

Petition of the Jewish Nation to the Honorable Lords, Directors of the Chartered West India Company (January 1655)

—Petition on behalf of the Jews in New Netherland

The merchants of the Portuguese Nation residing in this City respectfully remonstrate to your Honors that it has come to their knowledge that your Honors raise obstacles to the giving of permits or passports to the Portuguese Jews to travel and to go to reside in New Netherland, which if persisted in will result to the great disadvantage of the Jewish nation. It also can be of no advantage to the general Company but rather damaging. . . .

It is well known to your Honors that the Jewish nation in Brazil have at all times been faithful and have striven to guard and maintain that place, risking for that purpose their possessions and their blood. . . .

Your Honors should also consider that the Honorable Lords . . . have in political matters always protected and considered the Jewish nation as upon the same footing as all the inhabitants. . . .

Your Honors should also please consider that many of the Jewish nation are principal shareholders in the Company. They having always striven their best for the Company. . . .

Therefore the petitioners request . . . that your Honors be pleased not to exclude but to grant the Jewish nation passage to and residence in that country; otherwise this would result in a great prejudice to their reputation.

What reasons did the Jews of Amsterdam give for allowing the Jews of New Amsterdam to be allowed to live there? How convincing were they?

The Dutch West India Company directive to New Netherland

We would have liked to effectuate and fulfill your wishes and request that the new territories should no more be allowed to be infected by people of the Jewish nation, for we foresee therefrom the same difficulties which you fear, but after having further weighed and considered the matter, we observe that this would be somewhat unreasonable and unfair, especially because of the considerable loss sustained by this nation, with others in the taking of Brazil, as also because of the large amount of capital which they still have invested in the shares of this company. Therefore after many deliberations we have finally decided and resolved . . . that these people may travel and trade to and in New Netherland and live and remain there provided the poor among them shall not become a burden to the company or to the community, but be supported by their own nation. You will now govern yourself accordingly.

Why did the directors of the Dutch West India Company permit the Jews to settle in New Amsterdam? What do you think of their reasoning?

land" outside the city. By 1657, Jews had found business opportunities as merchants, importers, and exporters. By 1660, they were openly conducting religious services in a rented house.

IMPROVEMENTS UNDER THE BRITISH

In 1664, the British captured the Dutch colonies and divided New Amsterdam into New York and New Jersey. Now the Jews were subject to British law. They soon learned that British law made it difficult for **aliens** to participate in trade. Even though the law was not strictly enforced in the colonies, it was important for non-British immigrants to the colonies to become citizens of Great Britain. In England, **naturalization** required proof that one was Protestant. In the colonies, in order to encourage business and trade, naturalization was made easier. In 1667, the Treaty of Breda gave full rights of trade, worship, ownership of property, and inheritance to the settlers in New York, including the Jews. By 1700, Jews were allowed to vote and serve on juries. Between 1718 and 1739, at least thirteen Jews were naturalized in New York.

The Naturalization Act of 1740 encouraged immigration to the colonies and created organized procedures for naturalization. Now anyone who had been born in a British colony or had lived in a British colony for seven years was eligible for citizenship. Most important for the Jews, the law stated that one did not have to take a Protestant **sacrament,** and it removed the words "upon the true Faith of a Christian" from the oath that one had to swear. The new law made it easier for Jews to become naturalized citizens in the colonies than in England.

Aliens are not citizens of the country in which they reside.

Naturalization is the process by which one becomes a citizen of a country.

A **sacrament** is a Christian rite (a ceremonial act) believed to have been decreed by Jesus to symbolize, or confer, grace (the love of God).

Why was citizenship important to these Jews?

OTHER PLACES, OTHER BATTLES

While the Jews in New York (formerly New Amsterdam) were making progress, Jews in the other colonies had their own battles to fight. Each colony's laws were different, depending on the colony's founders and their beliefs. For years, Jews were not even permitted to live in Massachusetts, Connecticut, and New Hampshire.

Many colonial **charters** reflected the original settlers' goals and beliefs. The charter of Virginia, the first charter of an English settlement in America (in 1606), granted by King James I, declared that the colony was dedicated to furthering "the Christian Religion to such People as yet live in Darkness and miserable Ignorance of the true Knowledge and Worship of God." In 1639, the Fundamental Order of Connecticut, the first charter to be written by the colonists themselves, promised to "maintain and preserve the liberty and purity of the gospel of our Lord Jesus."

Charters are legal documents granting the right of settlement.

Maryland's Act Concerning Religion, created in 1649, promised freedom of religion, but only to those "professing to believe in Jesus Christ." Georgia's charter excluded only Catholics, but the colony's board of trustees recommended keeping Jews out, too. Finally, Governor James Oglethorpe raised no objections, and forty-one Jews were eventually allowed to settle in that colony.

Are you surprised by the colonial charters? Why? Why not?

Circumstances were somewhat better for Jews in other colonies. Some colonies gave Jews the right to vote—but none allowed a Jew to hold office. The Charter of Rhode Island (1663) and the Pennsylvania Charter of Privileges (1701) still mentioned Christianity. However, they also gave some, if not full, rights to non-Christians. These were important first steps toward granting Jews and other minority groups in the British colonies individual rights and guarantees of religious liberty.

By 1776, Jews could settle in any one of the thirteen colonies. There were no restrictions on where they could live and no rules governing the jobs they could hold. Jews in New York and Rhode Island were even allowed to attend universities—a right that was rare in Europe, where most Jews were also denied the right to own land or practice law or medicine. Although few took advantage of it, Jews gradually gained the right to hold public office without taking a Christian oath.

The Jews in the colonies had come a long way. No longer were they penniless wanderers fleeing country after country. They had fought intolerance and prejudice, and they had won many rights in their new homeland.

As Jews in America, we sometimes take our rights for granted. Now you know the hurdles that the early Jewish colonial settlers had to overcome. How does this knowledge affect you today?

Asser Levy: He fought for his rights . . . and won.

Asser Levy, an Ashkenazic Jew who was originally from Vilna, in Lithuania, arrived in New Amsterdam in 1654. He was penniless and soon began a protest against Governor Stuyvesant's imposition of a military-exemption tax on Jews. All Jewish men between the ages of 16 and 60 were taxed rather than asked to take their turn on guard duty. Levy could not afford to pay the tax and wanted to serve on guard duty instead. The Dutch leaders feared that other settlers would resent serving with a Jew. Levy's request was refused, but he appealed the decision. It took two years, but he finally won and was permitted to serve on guard duty. He once marched with the local militia against the Algonquian Indians.

Next, Levy decided to fight for citizenship. He gained the support of wealthy Jews in the colony and won again. At that point, Jews in New Amsterdam were given the right to citizenship, or burghership, as it was called.

Levy worked hard at a wide variety of jobs, from butcher to trader to merchant. As a butcher, he was excused from killing hogs because of his religious beliefs. In 1661, he became the first Jew in New Amsterdam to own his own house. He may have been the first Jewish property owner in the colonies.

When the English captured New Amsterdam and renamed it New York, Levy swore an oath of allegiance to the British king. All the rights he had under the Dutch were granted to him by the British. He was the first Jew to serve on a jury in North America.

When he died, court records show, his possessions included a pistol and a sword, a Sabbath lamp, a kiddush cup, and a spice box for **havdalah.** In recognition of his achievements, a public school in Manhattan and a park in Brooklyn, New York, are named for him. Although he began life in the colonies as a poor refugee, he became a well-known businessman and a fighter for religious equality and Jewish rights.

Havdalah is the ceremony performed on Saturday evening to mark the end of Shabbat.

What do the items listed in the court records tell you about Levy as an early American settler and as a Jew? Why was Levy an important example to the Jewish colonists? Is there one of his battles that you think was particularly important? Why?

Learn more about becoming a citizen. Do you know anyone who is a naturalized citizen? Ask him or her about the experience.

Becoming a U.S. citizen

The following information is summarized from the U.S. Bureau of Citizenship and Immigration Services website. Use a search engine like Google to locate the U.S. Bureau of Citizenship and Immigration Services website. When you find the site, select "Naturalization."

The general requirements for naturalization include:

- a period of continuous residence and physical presence in the United States

- an ability to read, write, and speak English

- a knowledge and understanding of U.S. history and government

- good moral character

- an attachment to the principles of the U.S. Constitution

- a favorable disposition toward the United States

Do the requirements and procedures for becoming a citizen surprise you? Do they seem fair? If you were writing the conditions and procedures, what would you include? Make a list below.

Step 1:

Submit a complete and accurate application form with all the necessary attachments and requirements. You must ensure that the application is submitted to the correct immigration office.

Step 2:

Prepare for the multiple-choice examination, which will include questions about U.S. history and government structure and will test English proficiency.

Step 3:

Prepare for the citizenship interview with an immigration officer.

Test yourself on U.S. history online at the U.S. Bureau of Citizenship and Immigration Services website. Could you pass the test?

Step 4:

Await immigration approval and the date of the naturalization ceremony.

Additional documents may be required. If your application is approved, you will be required to take the oath of allegiance to the United States in order to become a citizen.

Read the oath online at the U.S. Bureau of Citizenship and Immigration Services website.

_____

_____

_____

_____

_____

_____

From the Charter of Rhode Island and Providence Plantations, 1663

Now know bee, that wee beinge willinge to encourage the hopefull undertakeinge of oure sayd lovall and loveinge subjects, and to secure them in the free exercise and enjoyment of all theire civill and religious rights, appertaining to them, as our loveing subjects; and to preserve unto them that libertye, in the true Christian ffaith and worshipp of God, which they have sought with soe much travaill, and the peaceable myndes . . . and because some of the people and inhabitants of the same colonie cannot, in theire private opinions, conforme to the publique exercise of religion, according to the litturgy, formes and ceremonyes of the Church of England . . . Have therefore though ffit, and doe hereby publish, graunt, ordeyne and declare, That our royall will and pleasure is, that noe person within the sayd colonye, at any tyme hereafter, shall bee any wise molested, punished, disquieted, or called in question, for any differences in opinione in matters of religion . . . but that all and everye person and persons may, from tyme to tyme, and at all tymes hereafter, freelye and fullye have and enjoye his and theire owne judgments and consciences, in matter of religious concernments, throughout the tract of lande hereafter mentioned; they behaving themselves peaceablie and quietlie . . . And that they may bee in the better capacity to defend themselves, in theire just rights and libertyes against all the enemies of the Christian ffaith.

Create a charter

Read the excerpts from the charters of the colonies of Rhode Island and Virginia. If you were helping to write a charter for a new colony, what would you include? Make your list below.

_____

_____

_____

_____

_____

_____

_____

_____

_____

_____

_____

_____

_____

_____

From the First Charter of Virginia, 1606

Whereas our loving and well-disposed Subjects . . . have been humble Suitors unto us, that We would vouchsafe unto them our Licence, to make Habitation, Plantation, and to deduce a colony of sundry of our People into that part of America commonly called Virginia . . . We, greatly commending, and graciously accepting of, their Desires for the Furtherance of so noble a Work, which may, by the Providence of Almighty God, hereafter tend to the Glory of his Divine Majesty, in propagating of Christian Religion to such People, as yet live in Darkness and miserable Ignorance of the true Knowledge and Worship of God, and may in time bring the Infidels and Savages, living in those parts, to human Civility, and to a settled and quiet Government: Do, by these our Letters Patents, graciously accept of, and agree to, their humble and well-intended Desires.

Jewish communities in the colonies

On the map, highlight the areas with large Jewish populations in colonial times. Are there still large Jewish communities in these areas today?

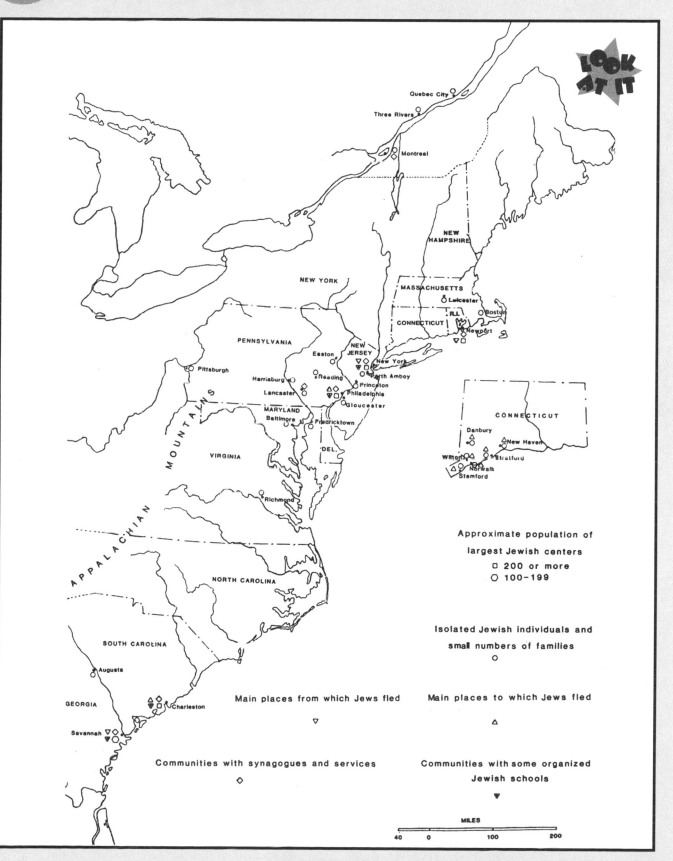

CHAPTER 3

THE POWER OF RELIGION

From the very beginning, religion was important to the Jews who settled in the New World. It had an effect on almost every aspect of their lives. Also, their lives in the colonies shaped the way they practiced Judaism.

THE COMMUNITY IS EVERYTHING

Just like in the Old World, the synagogue was the center of the Jewish community in the American colonies. The synagogue took care of everything about Jewish life—from prayer services to dietary laws, from life-cycle events to contact with other Jews around the world. The synagogue provided education for the children, buried the dead, and collected *tzedakah*. It was the meeting place for all the Jews in the community and was even responsible for activities like baking *matzah* and distributing *haroset* at Passover.

Tzedakah comes from the Hebrew word *tzedek*, which means "righteousness." *Tzedakah* is an obligation, something Jews are required to do.

What makes a Jewish community Jewish?

The symbol that marked a Jewish community as Jewish was the Torah. Having a Torah of its own created a "sacred space" for that group of Jews. It turned a rented building or a private home into a synagogue. A Torah scroll first arrived in New Amsterdam in 1655 from Holland. Only eight years later, the Torah was returned because the community had scattered. When the British took control of New York, another Torah was brought to the New World, and the Jewish community started to worship together again in private. (Jews in North America were able to begin to worship publicly around the turn of the eighteenth century.) Wherever Jews created communities in the New World, they either brought Torahs with them or borrowed them from established congregations.

from Jonathan D. Sarna, *American Judaism: A History* (New Haven: Yale University Press, 2004)

THINK ABOUT IT

What are some of the symbols, structures, and institutions that make a community Jewish today?

The synagogue helped encourage a feeling of Jewish tradition and togetherness. It efficiently met the religious needs of each small group of Jewish colonists, who lived far from other Jews. This all-encompassing kind of synagogue made the communities' survival more likely.

TRADITION, TRADITION

When the Jews of New York formed their congregation, Shearith Israel, they met in a small rented house on Mill Street. Today, Mill Street is called South William Street, but it was known then as Jews' Alley. Tradition was important. At Shearith Israel, congregants still said some prayers in Portuguese, the language of the congregation's founders. The minutes of their business meetings were written in Portuguese (with an English translation), even though only a few congregants understood the language. The congregation also followed prayer rituals that were practiced by Portuguese Jews and used the Portuguese melodies. Changes were forbidden. The congregation wanted every member of its "nation" (what the Portuguese Jews called themselves) to feel at home in any Sephardic synagogue anywhere in the world.

Custom among the Sephardic Jews—one that was also practiced by many non-Jewish colonists—was fully obeying the officers and elders of the congregation. Jews in the colonies did not have the right to disagree with their leaders or to challenge the leadership in a free election. They were not permitted to leave the congregation and found a new one. They could not practice their Judaism

The power to punish

Trying to punish a member of the community required community cooperation. The leaders of Shearith Israel found this out the hard way. They tried to crack down on members who were known to "dayly violate the principles [of] our holy religion, such as Trading on the Sabath, Eating of forbidden Meats & other Henious Crimes." The elders, who made up the governing board of the congregation, called the *adjunta*, quoted the Bible and threatened these people. The accused were even told that "when Dead [they] will not be buried according to the manner of our brethren." But, within six months, there was so much opposition that the congregational leaders changed their minds. They quoted Isaiah who said to "open the gates" (26:2), and welcomed everyone back into the community.

from Jonathan D. Sarna, *American Judaism: A History* (New Haven: Yale University Press, 2004)

 Do you think a synagogue should be able to punish members for not following religious laws?

independently, but they did not mind. In fact, they would have thought such ideas dangerous to the community and even to Judaism. All the power was held by the *yehidim*, wealthy men who supported the congregation and had status in the community. The rest of the congregation, including women, had seats in the synagogue but no authority at all.

 How do you feel when you go to a synagogue where the prayers and rituals are different from your own?

In the synagogue

Seating arrangements in the synagogues in New York and Newport demonstrated the inequalities within those Jewish communities. The congregation assigned a "proper" place to every person, and there was a membership tax on each seat. In New York, members of one wealthy family, the Gomez clan, had the best seats and paid the highest tax. Other congregants paid less and sat farther from the ark. The women sat in a special section away from the men, according to Jewish tradition. This section was small, and in New York, where women attended services regularly, there were often arguments over the seats. Therefore, a special section was reserved for the women of the wealthy Gomez family.

SIMILARITIES TO THEIR CHRISTIAN NEIGHBORS

Another reason for the synagogue's authority was the colonial government's desire not to interfere with the way a synagogue was run. The government treated churches the same way. The synagogue had the power of *herem*, excommunication. This power meant that the leaders could expel from the community anyone who disobeyed the rules. Although excommunication hardly ever happened, mainly because congregants refused to cooperate and it was almost impossible to enforce, the threat was real. More often, punishments were fines, refusing someone an honor in the synagogue, and most severe of all, refusing burial in the Jewish cemetery.

Aaron Lopez, Newport merchant.

A rose by any other name

Some Sephardic Jews used different names for their synagogue lives and their business lives. Aaron Lopez, a well-known Newport merchant, used his Portuguese name, Duarte, in business and his Hebrew name, Aaron, in synagogue.

Do you have a Hebrew name? What is it? _____

Whom were you named for? _____

What does your name mean? _____

Find out the Hebrew names of some of your friends. Do they have biblical names? Israeli names? What do their names mean? List some Hebrew names and their meanings below.

Hebrew Name	English Meaning	Biblical Name	Israeli Name
_____	_____	☐	☐
_____	_____	☐	☐
_____	_____	☐	☐

Like many of their Christian neighbors, members of the Jewish community lacked professional leaders. The *parnas,* or president, was the leader of the congregation and the *ḥazan,* the cantor, chanted the prayers and performed many of the rituals. No synagogue hired a rabbi, called a **ḥacham** by the Sephardic Jews, until 1840, well after the American Revolution. There were probably several reasons for this: The synagogues had too few members and not enough money, and a rabbi would have had to have been brought from Europe. In fact, many rabbis might not have wanted to come to America—a frontier with only small Jewish communities. But only a few of the Christian churches had professional leaders; the Jews were not alone. Finally, because the community was becoming so diverse—with both Sephardim and Ashkenazim from many lands—it would have been hard to find a leader who would satisfy everyone.

 A **ḥacham** is a wise or learned person. The word comes from *ḥochmah,* Hebrew for "wisdom."

 What are some examples of diversity in the Jewish community today? What is positive about diversity? What can be the challenges of diversity? How diverse is your synagogue? your Jewish community?

DIFFERENCES AND AGREEMENT

The diversity of the community made for difficulties. The Ashkenazic and Sephardic Jews had very different backgrounds and traditions. In most other places in the world, they lived and worshipped separately. Not in the colonies. In North America, Jews worshipped together.

At first, the Sephardim had both religious and cultural authority. But by the 1720s, the power was slowly shifting to the Ashkenazim, who were by then in the majority. Some Ashkenazic Jews even became officers of their congregations and later established congregations of their own.

The Jewish colonists *did* agree on the importance of keeping Judaism and its central values strong. This conviction was demonstrated in the design of Shearith Israel's Mill Street synagogue, which was consecrated in

1730. The members of this congregation had never before built, or even owned, a synagogue. Now they had a chance to show what they felt strongly about. Around them they saw churches with elaborate buildings with beautiful towers and spires—certain displays of the colonists' wealth. The Jewish colonists had also been financially successful and could have designed a comparably elaborate building. Instead, the new synagogue was plain on the outside. Inside, it emphasized Sephardic tradition. Why? The congregants did not want to draw too much attention to themselves, but they did want to glorify Judaism.

 Think about synagogues you know. What do their architecture and design show about the people who built them?

Learn about the differences between Ashkenazic and Sephardic synagogues and traditions. If you can, visit an Ashkenazic and a Sephardic synagogue in your community. Is your synagogue Sephardic or Ashkenazic?

MINGLING WITH THEIR CHRISTIAN NEIGHBORS

While the synagogue played an important role in the lives of the Jewish colonists, the synagogue community in the New World did not control what congregants did in the secular (nonreligious) aspects of their lives the way synagogues did in Europe. They did not tax congregants' businesses or try to control what congregants said or did outside the synagogue. They did not punish congregants for dishonesty in business or in their personal lives. The Jews lived among their Christian neighbors and had many social and business interactions with them. They began to feel comfortable interacting with them, starting businesses together and visiting Christians' homes—something that was rare in the Old World.

Some Jews and Christians even fell in love and married, a phenomenon that alarmed the Jewish community. However, it was a sign of the Jews' acceptance by their neighbors, since only a few Jews converted to Christianity in order to marry a Christian. Some intermarried Jews drifted away from the Jewish community sooner or later, but others did not. And they were permitted to remain in the community. Even though Jewish tradition is strict on the subject of intermarriage, the society in which the colonists lived was not. Jews in North America were caught between Jewish law and the Christian society in which they lived—and the conflict was difficult for them.

The Jewish colonists were caught in other ways as well. Local laws prohibited working on Sunday, the Christian Sabbath. If Jews did not work on Shabbat, they had only a five-day workweek. Jewish holidays were difficult to observe for the same reason. Keeping kosher made it hard, and even embarrassing, for some people to travel or eat anywhere except at home. Jews solved these dilemmas in different ways, as you will read in the box below, making the community even more diverse. Within the community—and even within families—some Jews continued to be very observant while others did not.

The changes within the colonial Jewish community made it different from other Jewish communities around the world—and similar to other minority religious communities in the colonies. Even though the colonial Jews still felt strong ties to one another and to Jews around the world, their community had a character all its own.

 Are there ways in which Jews today feel tension between Jewish laws and traditions and the laws and traditions of secular American society? Do you feel those tensions? How do you handle them?

A Shabbat dilemma—and how a colonist handled it

Some of the Jewish colonists observed Shabbat strictly while others did not. Here is an account of a man named David McClure, who was a missionary to the Delaware Indians. In 1772, he spent a weekend in Lancaster, Pennsylvania, and on a Saturday went to the home of Joseph Simon, a well-known local Jewish merchant, with a business order.

Simon said,

"Gentlemen, today is my Sabbath, & I do not do business in it; if you will please to call tomorrow, I will wait on you." We observed that the same reasons which prevented his payment of the order on that day would prevent our troubling him the day following [Sunday]. We apologized for our intruding on his Sabbath, & told him we would wait until Monday. He replied, you are on a journey, & it may be inconvenient to you to wait. He went to call in his neighbor, Dr. Boyd, & took from his Desk a bag, laid it on the table & presented the order to the Dr. The doctor counted out the money and we gave a recipt. The Jew sat looking on, to see that all was rightly transacted, but said nothing, & thus quieted his conscience against the rebuke of a violation of his Sabbath.

from "Lancaster in 1772," *Journal of the Lancaster County Historical Society* 5 (1901): 108–9.

THINK ABOUT IT Do you make a special effort to observe Shabbat? How?

A nation or part of American society?

In the beginning, the Jews of the New World thought of themselves, like other Sephardic Jews around the world, as members of the Jewish or Portuguese "Nation." After they had lived in North America with members of other minority groups for awhile, they began to call themselves members of a "religious society" just as the Christian religious societies like the Quakers—the "Society of Friends"—spoke of themselves. When Ezekiel Levy was hired in 1774 in Philadelphia to serve as a teacher, *shohet,* and reader, his contract was with the "Jewish Society" of the city. Before that time, contracts had read "the Jewish Nation." When the Jews of New York wrote a letter of welcome to Governor George Clinton, in 1783, they used the same term. They were demonstrating the new way that they thought of themselves and that Judaism stood equal with other religions in the New World. They were also concerned about being part of the larger society in America.

from Jonathan D. Sarna, *American Judaism: A History* (New Haven: Yale University Press, 2004)

 A *shohet* is someone who slaughters and prepares kosher meat according to Jewish law (*halachah*).

 Are Jews today a religious group or a nation?

 ## Crossword puzzle

Use what you learned in Chapters 1–3 to complete the crossword puzzle.

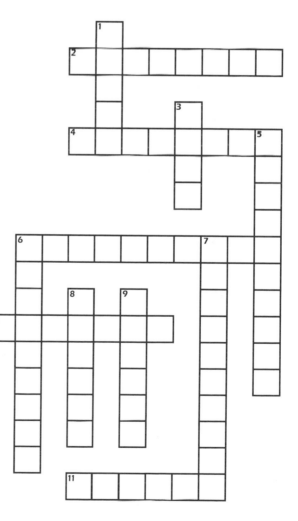

ACROSS

2. An explorer who sailed the ocean blue
4. A Jew who converted to Christianity
6. The governor of New Amsterdam who did not want Jews to settle there
10. A legal document granting the right of settlement
11. Hebrew for "wise person"

DOWN

1. The oldest synagogue still standing in North America
3. Colonist who fought for his rights
5. The governor of Georgia who finally allowed the Jews to settle in his colony
6. Spanish and Portuguese Jews
7. Jews from Central Europe
8. A Jewish woman who wrote letters giving motherly advice to her son
9. The city in Brazil where Jews settled

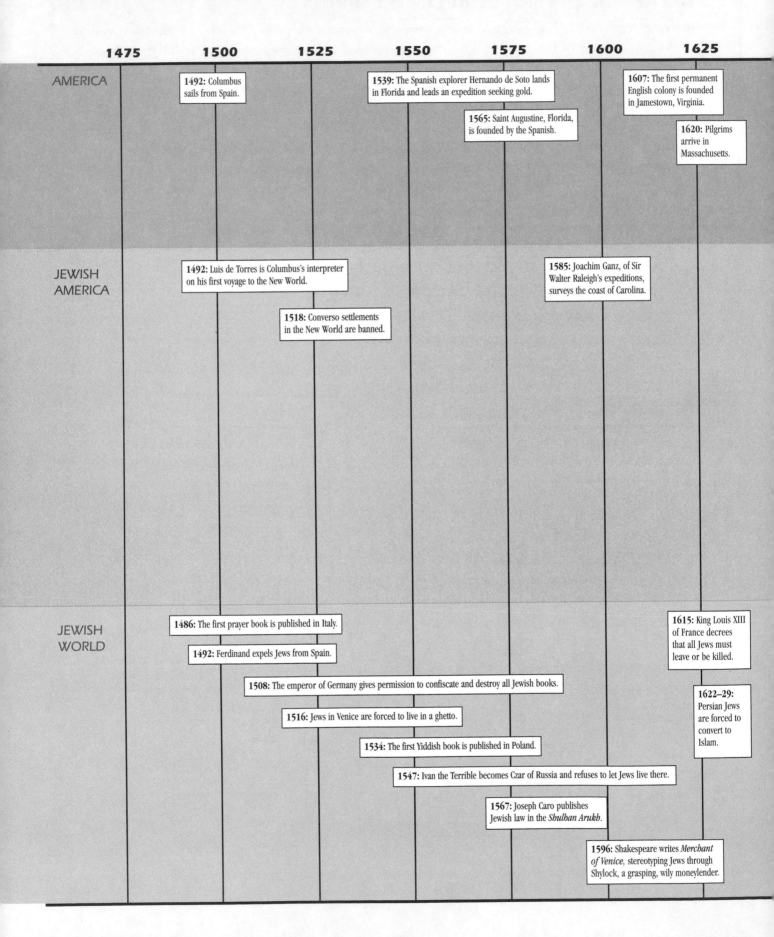

	1475	1500	1525	1550	1575	1600	1625

AMERICA

1492: Columbus sails from Spain.

1539: The Spanish explorer Hernando de Soto lands in Florida and leads an expedition seeking gold.

1565: Saint Augustine, Florida, is founded by the Spanish.

1607: The first permanent English colony is founded in Jamestown, Virginia.

1620: Pilgrims arrive in Massachusetts.

JEWISH AMERICA

1492: Luis de Torres is Columbus's interpreter on his first voyage to the New World.

1518: Converso settlements in the New World are banned.

1585: Joachim Ganz, of Sir Walter Raleigh's expeditions, surveys the coast of Carolina.

JEWISH WORLD

1486: The first prayer book is published in Italy.

1492: Ferdinand expels Jews from Spain.

1508: The emperor of Germany gives permission to confiscate and destroy all Jewish books.

1516: Jews in Venice are forced to live in a ghetto.

1534: The first Yiddish book is published in Poland.

1547: Ivan the Terrible becomes Czar of Russia and refuses to let Jews live there.

1567: Joseph Caro publishes Jewish law in the *Shulḥan Arukh*.

1596: Shakespeare writes *Merchant of Venice*, stereotyping Jews through Shylock, a grasping, wily moneylender.

1615: King Louis XIII of France decrees that all Jews must leave or be killed.

1622–29: Persian Jews are forced to convert to Islam.

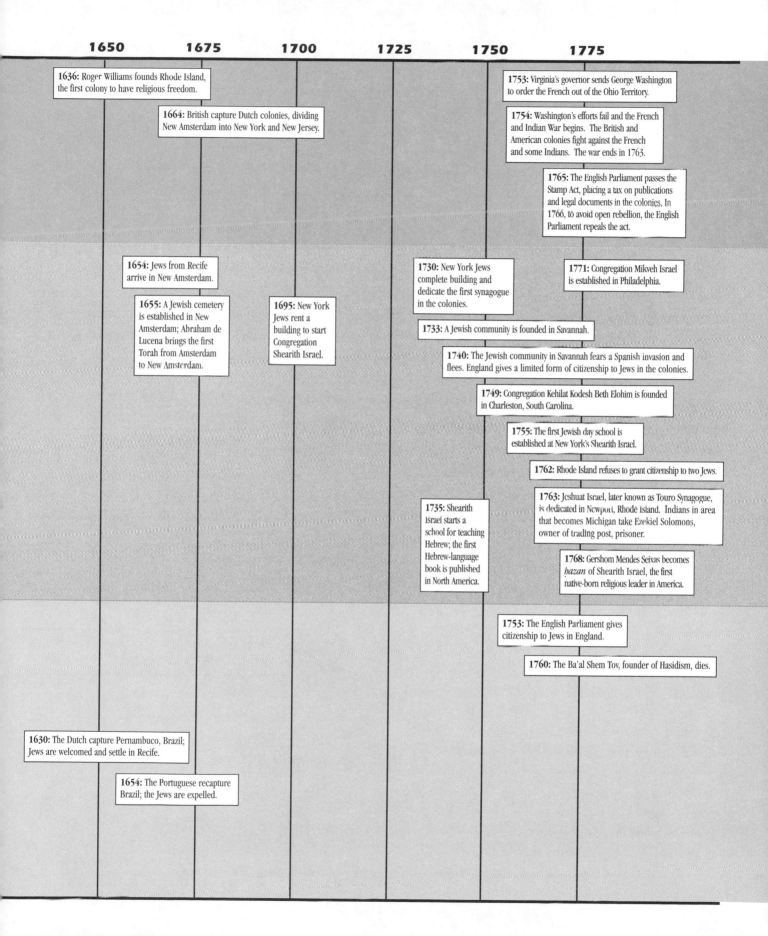

1650   **1675**   **1700**   **1725**   **1750**   **1775**

1636: Roger Williams founds Rhode Island, the first colony to have religious freedom.

1664: British capture Dutch colonies, dividing New Amsterdam into New York and New Jersey.

1753: Virginia's governor sends George Washington to order the French out of the Ohio Territory.

1754: Washington's efforts fail and the French and Indian War begins. The British and American colonies fight against the French and some Indians. The war ends in 1763.

1765: The English Parliament passes the Stamp Act, placing a tax on publications and legal documents in the colonies, In 1766, to avoid open rebellion, the English Parliament repeals the act.

1654: Jews from Recife arrive in New Amsterdam.

1655: A Jewish cemetery is established in New Amsterdam; Abraham de Lucena brings the first Torah from Amsterdam to New Amsterdam.

1695: New York Jews rent a building to start Congregation Shearith Israel.

1730: New York Jews complete building and dedicate the first synagogue in the colonies.

1771: Congregation Mikveh Israel is established in Philadelphia.

1733: A Jewish community is founded in Savannah.

1740: The Jewish community in Savannah fears a Spanish invasion and flees. England gives a limited form of citizenship to Jews in the colonies.

1749: Congregation Kehilat Kodesh Beth Elohim is founded in Charleston, South Carolina.

1755: The first Jewish day school is established at New York's Shearith Israel.

1762: Rhode Island refuses to grant citizenship to two Jews.

1735: Shearith Israel starts a school for teaching Hebrew; the first Hebrew-language book is published in North America.

1763: Jeshuat Israel, later known as Touro Synagogue, is dedicated in Newport, Rhode Island. Indians in area that becomes Michigan take Ezekiel Solomons, owner of trading post, prisoner.

1768: Gershom Mendes Seixas becomes *hazan* of Shearith Israel, the first native-born religious leader in America.

1753: The English Parliament gives citizenship to Jews in England.

1760: The Ba'al Shem Tov, founder of Hasidism, dies.

1630: The Dutch capture Pernambuco, Brazil; Jews are welcomed and settle in Recife.

1654: The Portuguese recapture Brazil; the Jews are expelled.

CHAPTER 4

FIGHTING AND FINANCING THE WAR

Why was the Revolutionary War important to the Jews of the American colonies?

"One if by land, two if by sea"—according to Henry Wadsworth Longfellow's famous poem "Paul Revere's Ride," this was the lantern signal that Revere would watch for in the tower of the Old North Church in Boston. It would alert him to ride through the night to warn colonists that British soldiers were approaching. Even though the poem is not accurate and Revere was stopped by British troops, Longfellow's lines convey the excitement of the beginning of the American Revolution and the start of a time of growth, opportunity, and freedom for Jews in the soon-to-be new country.

HOW DID IT COME TO THIS?

Life had been good for the Jews in the colonies under British rule. There were between 1,000 and 2,500 Jews, out of about 2.5 million people, living in the thirteen colonies by 1775. Generally, most of them had more rights than they had had in Europe. They were allowed to build synagogues and to worship as they wished. Many were making a good living. But conditions were not perfect. Some Jews still experienced discrimination, and in some colonies their rights were limited. For example, they were not allowed to vote or hold public office. They also knew that the rights of their friends and families who stayed in England were limited.

Many of the Jews in the colonies were businessmen and merchants. British laws and taxes hurt them just as much as they hurt their Christian neighbors. The colonists were not permitted to send representatives to Parliament. Their slogan became "No taxation without representation."

The 1765 Stamp Act required that a tax stamp be placed on all publications and legal documents. It caused the first major protest by the colonists. Of the 375 people who signed a resolution against it, 10 were Jewish. That tax was **repealed,** but the spirit of revolution had taken hold.

The British soon tried again with the Townshend Acts, which placed taxes on a variety of goods. Again Jewish merchants were among those to sign an agreement not to **import** or use these goods. The Townshend Acts were repealed, leaving only a tax on tea. Several Jewish merchants in New York joined their fellow colonists protesting that tax. British troops soon arrived in the colonies to help enforce Parliament's laws.

Repealed means "cancelled."

Import means "receive goods from foreign countries for sale or use."

Why was it important for Jewish colonists to protest British taxes?

THE BREAK

In 1770, British troops killed five colonists in a riot that came to be known as the Boston massacre. In 1773, during the Boston Tea Party, a group of colonists dressed as Indians threw a shipload of British tea into Boston Harbor. They did not want it to be unloaded because they would have had to pay a tax on it. The next year, Parliament decided to crack down on the colonists with even more laws that limited their freedom.

Nonetheless, the colonists were not ready to make a final break with England. They agreed to send delegates to Philadelphia in September of 1774 to attend the Continental Congress. The Congress wrote a declaration saying that the colonists would obey certain acts of Parliament—those that were in their best interests—but would disobey others, such as certain taxes. Even so, the relationship between the colonies and Britain worsened.

 Why do you think it was so hard for the colonists to break with England? Do you think it was especially hard for the Jewish colonists? Why?

The British did not believe that the colonists would offer much resistance, so they sent troops to Concord, Massachusetts, to capture the military supplies stored there. The night the troops arrived, Paul Revere and his comrades made their famous ride. When several hundred red-coated troops arrived in Lexington, Massachusetts, at dawn on April 19, 1775, seventy colonial militiamen were waiting for them. A shot was fired, the British fired several volleys, and eight colonists were killed. The British then marched to Concord, five miles away, where a larger group of colonists was waiting. This time, British blood was spilled, and colonists hid in the woods waiting to ambush British soldiers as they marched in columns along the road back to Boston. By the end of the first day of the American Revolution, the British had suffered 272 injuries; the Americans, just 93.

On July 4, 1776, the Second Continental Congress, meeting in Philadelphia, adopted the Declaration of Independence. Fighting spread throughout the colonies, and British soldiers occupied New York and Newport, Rhode Island, among other cities. The Jews, like the other colonists, had to choose whether to stay in their homes or flee to cities controlled by the supporters of independence.

JEWISH LOYALISTS AND JEWISH PATRIOTS

According to John Adams, and other observers at the time, the colonists' loyalties were divided. One-third supported independence, one-third wanted to remain loyal to England, and one-third were undecided. Colonists who favored independence called themselves Patriots or Whigs, after the opposition party in England. Those who remained loyal to the king were called Loyalists or Tories, named for the ruling political party in Britain.

The Declaration of Independence and the Bible

The Declaration of Independence states,

We hold these truths to be self-evident, that all men are created equal, that they are endowed by their Creator with certain unalienable rights, that among these are life, liberty, and the pursuit of happiness.

 Unalienable, or **inalienable,** means "something that cannot be transferred, or given away, to another person."

What rights that you have as an American are most important to you? List them below.

_____

_____

_____

In Genesis, it says that people are created *b'tzelem Elohim* ("in the image of God"). What does this mean to you? Write a few of your ideas below. How does this idea influence your reading of the lines from the Declaration of Independence? How does it affect your behavior toward other people and toward the world (for example, the environment)?

_____

_____

_____

_____

_____

_____

_____

_____

_____

_____

_____

Do It

Look at the map of "Jewish communities in colonies" (page 15). Find the major communities that had synagogues and held religious services. Locate the communities that Jews left and the communities to which they went. Do some research on one of these Jewish communities, and teach what you learn to your class. Find out when the oldest synagogue in your community was founded.

Most Jewish colonists, especially those who had been born in the colonies, supported independence. Those who were merchants thought that independence was in their best interests. Many Jews believed in the liberal ideals of the Revolution, and they appreciated the new, more accepting environment that it fostered. There were Jews on both sides of the battle, however. In fact, several colonial Jewish families were divided between the Loyalists and the Patriots.

Loyalists were mostly concerned with keeping life the way it was. They had more rights in the British-controlled colonies than their relatives had who stayed in Europe. They wanted to maintain the status quo—to keep the colonies as they were.

It was especially difficult for Jewish businessmen to choose sides. Many had been hit hard by the English taxes. But if they sided with the patriots and the king's forces won the war, businesses in England might not trade with them after the war.

 THINK ABOUT IT Would you have been a loyalist or a patriot? Why?

THE WAR IN NEWPORT

The Rhode Island Assembly passed a law saying that anyone who was thought to sympathize with the British must swear loyalty to the Revolution. Four Jews were among the seventy-six men who were asked to take the oath. All four refused. One of them, Moses Michael Hays, was a patriot who refused because the oath included the words "upon the true faith of a Christian." After much discussion, those words were removed, and Hays signed his name.

The other three men—Isaac Hart, Meyer Polock, and Isaac Touro—were loyalists. Isaac Hart's family was especially friendly with the British. The Harts entertained British officers and even imported tea after the patriots had stopped accepting goods imported from England. Other

Hays and the loyalty oath

Moses Michael Hays signed one loyalty oath, as demanded by the Rhode Island Assembly, which said, "We . . . do solemnly and sincerely declare that we believe the war . . . in which the United American Colonies are now engaged against the fleets and armies of Great Britain is on the part of said colonies just and necessary . . . we will heartily assist in the defense of the United Colonies."

However, one month later, after the Declaration of Independence was signed, the Assembly asked him to sign another declaration of loyalty. This one was only required of people who were suspected of being enemies of the patriot cause. Hays refused to sign, although he was loyal, and said that he was only being accused because he was a Jew. He wrote: "I decline subscribing the test at present from these principles: . . . that I am an Israelite and am not allowed the liberty of a vote or voice in common with the rest of the voters."

from Jonathan D. Sarna, Benny Kraut, and Samuel K. Joseph, eds., *Jews and the Founding of the Republic* (New York: M. Wiener Publishing, 1985)

colonists grew resentful, and the Rhode Island legislature voted to strip the family of its rights and properties. Loyalists gave Hart property in New York, and before the war was over, he died defending a loyalist fortification in the battle of Long Island.

Isaac Touro, the *hazan* of the Newport synagogue, remained in Newport with his family until 1780. Then they, too, went to New York, where they lived on money given them by the British. Finally, they moved to Jamaica, where Touro died a year later.

Aaron Lopez, also of Newport, was a patriot whose family had lived as secret Jews in Portugal. An important shipowner, Lopez is said to have had thirty large ships and more than one hundred other boats. He was described by Ezra Stiles, a Christian minister and president of Yale University, as "a merchant of first eminence; for honor and extent of commerce probably surpassed by no merchant in America." Despite pressure from the British, Lopez allowed his ships to be used to help supply the Continental army. When the British attacked Newport, Lopez fled to Massachusetts. He drowned while watering his horse in a river when returning after the war.

The British occupied Newport from December 1776 until October 1779. Many people, including the Jews, fled the city. The Jewish community that was once so strong never was so strong again.

THE WAR COMES TO NEW YORK

When the British attacked New York in 1776, many residents left the city. Many who were loyal to the king, including some Jews, stayed behind.

One who fled the city was Gershom Mendes Seixas, Congregation Shearith Israel's religious leader, the first *hazan* born in the colonies. Although some loyalists in the congregation objected, he took the Torah and other religious objects with him. He went to Stratford, Connecticut, while most of the rest of the congregation went to Philadelphia. Four years later, he joined others there and helped found a new synagogue, Mikveh Israel. After the war, Seixas returned to Shearith Israel and, in 1789, was one of the clergymen who participated in the inauguration of George Washington as the new nation's first president.

 In 1776, a man named Hart Jacobs of New York, asked to be excused from fighting on Friday night because it was Shabbat. The Committee of Safety, the patriot authority, ordered that he be permitted not to fight on that night and that he perform his full tour of duty on other nights. What do you think of Jacobs' action? What do you think of the committee's decision? What does it tell you about the status of Jews in the colonies? What would you have done?

A patriot's sermon

Gershom Mendes Seixas, *hazan* of Shearith Israel, was the first Jewish religious leader to give his sermons in English. In one of them, Seixas prayed "to put in the heart of our Sovereign Lord, George the Third, and in the hearts of his Councellors, Princes and Servants, to turn away their fierce Wrath from our North America . . . . That there may no more blood be shed in these Countries, O Lord our God . . . . And that thou mayest send the Angels of mercy to proclaim Peace to all America and to the inhabitants thereof . . . ." During the Revolution, the Jews often gathered in their synagogues on days the Continental Congress set aside for fasting and prayer. This was seen as a sign of their patriotism. It was on one of these days that Seixas gave this sermon.

Fleeing the city

The Minute Book of Shearith Israel Synagogue has the following entry for 1783:

During the interval [from 1776 to 1783] most of the Yehidim [Members] had left the city in consequence of the Revolutionary War and the city having been taken possession of by the British troops, it was not until peace took place that the members returned to the city, when Mr. Hayman Levy called the meeting.

from Shearith Israel Archives

War and Shabbat: A dilemma?

Halachah emphasizes that with a few important exceptions, we must do whatever is necessary to save a life *(pikuah nefesh):* "The saving of life supersedes the Sabbath" (Babylonian Talmud, Shabbat 132a). In wartime, that may mean fighting on Shabbat and holidays.

The U.S. Department of Defense Directory "Accommodation of Religious Practices" states:

A basic principle of our nation is free exercise of religion. The Department of Defense places a high value on the rights of members of the Armed Forces to observe . . . their respective religions. It is DoD policy that requests for accommodation of religious practices should be approved by commanders when accommodation will not have an adverse impact on military readiness, unit cohesion, standards, or discipline.

The following goals are to be used by the Military Departments in the development of guidance . . . concerning the accommodation of religious practices. . . .

Worship services, holy days, and Sabbath observances should be accommodated, except when precluded by military necessity.

Based on these two pieces of information—about Jewish law and American military practice—write your position on fighting on Shabbat. Do you come to a different decision than Hart Jacobs did during the Revolution?

_____

_____

_____

_____

_____

_____

_____

_____

One New York Jew who volunteered to fight for the patriot cause was Isaac Franks. He was seventeen when he signed up to fight with Colonel Lasher's Volunteers of New York. He was wounded and taken prisoner during the battle of Long Island but escaped to New Jersey by paddling across the Hudson River in a leaky boat using only one paddle! He rejoined Washington's army and stayed with it for the next six years.

Another New Yorker who helped the patriot cause was Haym Salomon. Salomon had come to New York from Poland, where he had learned many languages. In New York, he became a successful businessman—and a member of the Sons of Liberty, a group of patriots who supported the Revolution. When the war started, the British arrested him for spying and helping to get food to the Continental army. But when they discovered he spoke German, he was freed and put to work as an interpreter for the German **mercenary** soldiers in the British army. Even so, he was also able to continue helping the colonists—he encouraged the German soldiers to desert.

A **mercenary** is a soldier who is paid to fight for a country other than his or her own.

When the British found out what he was doing, Salomon escaped again—this time to Philadelphia. Although he was penniless, he quickly got back into business—and into helping the Continental army. He worked as a merchant and **broker,** helping Robert Morris, the colonies' superintendent of finance, raise money for the army. Morris called him "the little Jewish broker." He was able to arrange loans for the colonies from France and Holland. He also lent money to officers in the army and members of the Continental Congress, including James Madison, a future president. Madison wrote to a friend, "the kindness of our little friend on Front Street near the Coffee House is a fund that will prevent me from extremities."

A **broker** works, for a fee, to negotiate an agreement, purchase, or sale.

Patriot and hero

In 1975, the U.S. Postal Service, as part of a series called "Contributors to the Cause," issued a commemorative stamp honoring Haym Salomon. The stamp was printed on the front and the back. On the glue side, these words were printed in green ink: "Financial Hero–Businessman and broker Haym Salomon was responsible for raising most of the money needed to finance the American Revolution and later to save the new nation from collapse." Even though Salomon did play an important role, most historians today believe that the claim that he "raised most of the money" for the Revolution is exaggerated.

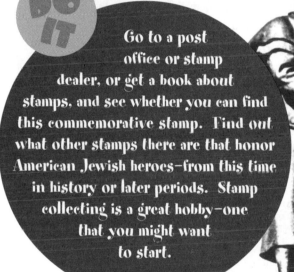

DO IT

Go to a post office or stamp dealer, or get a book about stamps, and see whether you can find this commemorative stamp. Find out what other stamps there are that honor American Jewish heroes—from this time in history or later periods. Stamp collecting is a great hobby—one that you might want to start.

ROBERT MORRIS · GEORGE WASHINGTON · HAYM SALOMON

★ ★ ★

THE GOVERNMENT OF THE UNITED STATES
WHICH GIVES TO BIGOTRY NO SANCTION · TO PERSECUTION
NO ASSISTANCE · REQUIRES ONLY THAT THEY WHO LIVE UNDER
ITS PROTECTION SHOULD DEMEAN THEMSELVES AS GOOD CITIZENS
IN GIVING IT ON ALL OCCASIONS THEIR EFFECTUAL SUPPORT
PRESIDENT GEORGE WASHINGTON 1790

★ ★ ★

Statue of Robert Morris, George Washington, and Haym Salomon on Wacker Drive in Chicago.

PHILADELPHIA JOINS IN

Many Jews from Philadelphia fought in the war. Benjamin Nones, who came from France, volunteered for the patriots and earned the rank of major in General Pulaski's Legion. He fought in almost every action that took place in South Carolina, until captured by the British. David Salisbury Franks became a major in the Continental army and was an aide to General Benedict Arnold. When Arnold took command of West Point, Franks went with him. And when Arnold was convicted of treason, Franks came under suspicion. Franks asked George Washington for a public hearing to clear his name. After the hearing, he was promoted and made diplomatic missions to Europe, first as a soldier and later as a civilian.

Solomon Bush, another Philadelphia Jew, joined the Pennsylvania militia and earned the rank of deputy adjutant general. He was wounded in a battle near Philadelphia and taken to his father's house for medical care. A loyalist informed the British, and he was captured. While imprisoned, Bush learned that a spy had infiltrated George Washington's staff. When the British paroled him to allow him to recover, he reported the information to Washington's staff.

Another Philadelphian, Phillip Moses Russell, joined the Continental army as a surgeon's mate. During the winter of 1777–1778, he served under George Washington at Valley Forge, helping the sick and wounded at camp hospitals, which were little more than shacks. In a letter, Washington commended him for giving "faithful attention to the sick and wounded" and showing "cool and collected deportment in battle."

Bush describes the war

Solomon Bush wrote this letter to a friend, telling about his wartime activities.

Dr Sir . . .

I suppose you heard of my being wounded the 18th of Sept' when with dificulty was bro' home in a most deplorable condition with my thigh broke and the surgeons pronounced my wound Mortal 7 days after the Enemy came . . . I was Concealed after the British Army came here 22 Days and shou'd have got Clear but a Vilain gave information of me when I was waited on by an officer what took my Parole when I wrote a line to the Commanding Officer letting him know of my being a prisoner and requesting a Surgeon which he imedeately Comply'd with and was attended every Day during their stay at this place; I am thank God getting better and have the Satisfaction to have my Limb perfectly Strait, my wishes are to be able to get Satisfaction and revenge the Rongs of my injured Country, I wish you joy of our Troops to the Northward and hope to tell you New York is ours before long. . . .

Your most affectionate Friend & Hbl Servt,
Solm Bush

from Jonathan D. Sarna, Benny Kraut and Samuel K. Joseph, eds., *Jews and the Founding of the Republic* (New York: M. Wiener Publishing, 1985)

Washington's landlord!

After the war, Isaac Franks went to Philadelphia, where he bought a large house outside the center of the town. In 1793, during a yellow-fever epidemic, President Washington was hesitant to go to Philadelphia, the capital at the time. He rented Franks' country house because "unquestionably Colonel Franks' (if to be had) would suit me best, because (it is) more commodious [roomy] for myself and the entertainment of company." Washington paid $66.66 for two months' rent.

DO IT

Do you live near the site of any famous Revolutionary War battlefields? Try to visit one and learn what happened there. If you can't visit, you can read about a site online, or write to one and request material.

THE JEWS OF THE SOUTH

Francis Salvador, the son of a wealthy London family, was the only Jew of the Revolutionary period to be elected to a state legislature, and he was the first Jew to die in the Revolution. He had settled in South Carolina, where he was elected to the First and Second South Carolina Provincial Congresses. He was also a financial adviser to the assembly, participated in a reorganization of the courts, helped to choose judges, and advised the assembly on election procedures. In 1776, he heard that Cherokee Indians, incited by the British, were attacking settlements. He and a group of friends hurried out to warn the settlers. Upon returning, he joined the militia in defending the settlements. During an attack by the Indians on the morning of August 1, he was shot, scalped, and left to die by the side of a road. His commanding officer found him. Salvador asked his friend whether he had beaten the enemy. When his friend answered that he had, Salvador said he was glad, and then said goodbye.

A Jewish hero

A plaque dedicated to Salvador's memory in Washington Square in Charleston reads,

Born an aristocrat, he became a democrat,
An Englishman, he cast his lot with America;
True to his ancient faith, he gave his life
For new hopes of human liberty and
understanding.

The Jewish community of Georgia also contributed to the Revolution. Philip Minis was active in Georgia's army and reportedly donated $11,000 to the troops. He and Levi Sheftall helped plan an attempt to recapture the city of Savannah from the British. The effort failed, and the British controlled the city until the end of the war.

Members of the Sheftall family, one of the first to settle in Savannah, played major roles during the war. Levi's half brother, Mordecai, was a colonel on the staff of the Georgia Brigade. He became commissary general for purchases and issues for the Continental troops in Georgia and South Carolina and made his son, Sheftall Sheftall, his assistant. Both father and son were captured by the British and held on a prison ship. They were exchanged for British prisoners and allowed to go to Philadelphia. Later, Sheftall Sheftall was the flag master of a ship that Washington sent under a flag of truce to Charleston, which was held by the British, to bring food, clothing, and money to American prisoners there.

THE WAR COMES TO A CLOSE

By 1779, the Americans' war effort had become too great for the British. The British general, Cornwallis, was waiting for fresh troops and supplies to arrive from England. In the meantime, General Washington had accepted an offer of help from the French. Before the British navy could arrive, Cornwallis was forced to surrender on October 19, 1781. Scattered fighting continued, but a temporary treaty was reached in 1782 and a final treaty came in 1783. It recognized the independence of the American colonies.

The Revolutionary War was over. Approximately 100 Jews had served in the military on the American side, either in state militias or in the Continental army. At times, Jews found themselves singled out because they were "different." But the Revolution was one of the first wars in modern times in which Jews were allowed to participate. They gave their talent, their money, and even their lives for their country.

What would you be willing to give for your country in time of war? Your money? Your life? Why or why not?

In the Jewish-American Hall of Fame, there are biographical sketches of many of the people mentioned in this book. Go to www.amuseum.org and take a virtual tour.

CHAPTER 5

BUILDING A NATION

How did the rights and privileges of citizenship in the new nation affect American Jews?

The Revolution was over. The United States of America was a free and independent nation. The Declaration of Independence set the tone for the new country's treatment of members of minority religions. Unlike other nations, America would not deny any religious group full citizenship. This principle had been a rallying cry of the Revolution, and the push for equal rights did not end there.

FREEDOM FROM THE BEGINNING

At first, the Congress of the **Confederation** governed the new nation. In 1787, as Americans began to settle the lands northwest of the Ohio River, it approved laws that laid out the government of the Ohio Territory. Those laws, known as the Northwest **Ordinance,** declared that settlers in the territory should not be discriminated against on account of their religion. From its beginning, the new nation stood by the spirit of the Revolution.

Confederate means "to unite in a partnership." March 1, 1781 is the date that the Articles of Confederation were adopted. The original thirteen states were united in a **confederation** from 1781–1789.

An **ordinance** is a law.

That same year, the country's leaders met to replace the Articles of Confederation with a stronger government. They wrote a constitution that would serve as a framework for a federal government, one with the power to enforce the laws of the nation, one that other governments would recognize as a strong, unified nation rather than a collection of separate states, each following its own path.

The Constitutional Convention met in Philadelphia from May to September, with George Washington presiding. The convention voted to keep its debates secret, and the new nation's Jews were not sure what to expect. Jonas Phillips, a German Jewish patriot who had moved to Philadelphia

during the Revolution rather than live under British rule in New York, submitted a letter to the convention. In it, he made a case for freedom of religion—and for equal rights for the Jews of America. American Jews—a very small minority in the United States—believed that they had earned these rights because of their service during the Revolution. Phillips was especially concerned about the religious requirements for holding office. He asked that the convention allow Jews to "think them self happy to live under a government where all Relegious societys are on an Eaquel footing." The Constitutional Convention did just that.

AMERICA'S CONSTITUTION AND AMERICA'S JEWS

Article VI of the Constitution states that "no religious test shall ever be required as a qualification to any office" in the new government. This means that any candidate can be elected to any government office without having to swear to his or her religious beliefs. One must only swear to obey and uphold the Constitution.

The First Amendment to the Constitution declares that Congress may never make a law that establishes a state religion or prevents the people from following whatever religion they want in any way they choose to observe it. This idea—the separation of church and state—gave America's Jews new opportunities and freedom. In fact, it was the first time that a national government had given Jews full citizenship since the Roman emperor Caracalla had done so, in 212 CE.

A patriot's letter

I ...being one of the people called Jews of the City of Philadelphia ...do behold with Concern that among the laws in the Constitution of Pennsylvania, there is a Clause ... —I do believe in one God the Creature and governour of the universe the Rewarder of the good & the punisher of the wicked—and I do acknowledge the scriptures of the old & New testament to be given by devine inspiration— to swear & believe that the new testament was given by devine inspiration is absolutely against the religious principle of a Jew and is against his Conscience to take any such oath—By the above law a Jew is deprived of holding any publick office ...which is Contredictory to the bill of Right Section 2 ...["nor can any man who acknowledges the being of a God be justly deprived ...of any civil right as a Citizen on account of his religious sentiments"].

It is well known ...that the Jews have been true and faithfull whigs, & during the late Contest with England they ...have bravely faught and bleed for liberty which they Can not Enjoy—Therefore if the honourable Convention shall in ther Wisdom ... alter the ...oath ...then the Israeletes will think them self happy to live under a government where all Relegious societys are on an Eaqual footing— I solecet this favour for my self my children & posterity, & for ...all the Isrealetes through the 13 united States of America. ...

Your Most devoted obed. Servant Jonas Phillips Philadelphia, 24th Ellul or Sepr 7th 1787

from *Publications of the American Jewish Historical Society 2* **(1894)**

THINK ABOUT IT — What does Phillips propose in his letter?

DO IT — Compare the ideas in Article VI of the Constitution discussed on this page with the First Amendment on page 34. Prepare an argument explaining why the First Amendment was an important addition to the Constitution.

The inspiration for the laws governing freedom of religion can be seen in earlier documents. In 1779, Thomas Jefferson introduced in the Virginia legislature a bill for religious freedom. It declared that all Virginians could acknowledge their religion without losing their liberty and that churches could not force members to contribute money. The bill did not pass, but during the debate, Jefferson made his beliefs clear.

In 1784, in Virginia, Patrick Henry sponsored a bill requiring taxpayers to pay for "Teachers of the Christian Religion." Christians would be able to say which church should receive their money, but non-Christians' taxes could not be used for non-Christian education. Henry's bill was defeated, and Jefferson's 1779 bill was reintroduced as the Act for Establishing Religious Freedom. It became law in 1786.

One of the most important delegates to the Constitutional Convention was James Madison. In fact, Madison has been called the Father of the Constitution. Before the convention began, he looked at more than 200 books on government, studying what made some governments successful and others unsuccessful. One principle he realized was that one group of citizens should not "invade the rights" of another. Thus, the delegates wrote in Article VI of the U.S. Constitution that there would be no religious requirement for holding elected office and that there would be no state religion. They also wrote in that same article that officials would be allowed to **affirm**—instead of swear—their oaths of office. Jefferson and many others were pleased with the Constitution, but they wanted the document to include laws that promised individual rights—including freedom of religion and the freedom to not practice any religion at all. In 1791, the first ten amendments to the Constitution—the Bill of Rights—were approved, guaranteeing those rights.

LEARN IT — **Affirm** means "to declare solemnly, without taking an oath."

THINK ABOUT IT — Why is it important to have freedom of religion and the freedom not to follow any religion?

The Bill of Rights

AMENDMENT I

Congress shall make no law respecting an establishment of religion, or prohibiting the free exercise thereof; or abridging the freedom of speech, or of the press; or the right of the people peaceably to assemble, and to petition the Government for a redress of grievances.

AMENDMENT II

A well regulated Militia, being necessary to the security of a free State, the right of the people to keep and bear Arms, shall not be infringed.

AMENDMENT III

No Soldier shall, in time of peace be quartered in any house, without the consent of the Owner, nor in time of war, but in a manner to be prescribed by law.

AMENDMENT IV

The right of the people to be secure in their persons, houses, papers, and effects, against unreasonable searches and seizures, shall not be violated, and no Warrants shall issue, but upon probable cause, supported by Oath or affirmation, and particularly describing the place to be searched, and the persons or things to be seized.

AMENDMENT V

No person shall be held to answer for a capital, or otherwise infamous crime, unless on a presentment or indictment of a Grand Jury, except in cases arising in the land or naval forces, or in the Militia, when in actual service in time of War or public danger; nor shall any person be subject for the same offence to be twice put in jeopardy of life or limb; nor shall be compelled in any criminal case to be a witness against himself, nor be deprived of life, liberty, or property, without due process of law; nor shall private property be taken for public use, without just compensation.

AMENDMENT VI

In all criminal prosecutions, the accused shall enjoy the right to a speedy and public trial, by an impartial jury of the State and district wherein the crime shall have been committed, which district shall have been previously ascertained by law, and to be informed of the nature and cause of the accusation; to be confronted with the witnesses against him; to have compulsory process for obtaining witnesses in his favor, and to have the assistance of Counsel for his defence.

AMENDMENT VII

In suits at common law, where the value in controversy shall exceed twenty dollars, the right of trial by jury shall be preserved, and no fact tried by a jury, shall be otherwise reexamined in any Court of the United States, than according to the rules of the common law.

AMENDMENT VIII

Excessive bail shall not be required, nor excessive fines imposed, nor cruel and unusual punishments inflicted.

AMENDMENT IX

The enumeration in the Constitution, of certain rights, shall not be construed to deny or disparage others retained by the people.

AMENDMENT X

The powers not delegated to the United States by the Constitution, nor prohibited by it to the States, are reserved to the States respectively, or to the people.

Know your rights

Read the Bill of Rights of the Constitution of the United States of America. How would you feel if any of these rights were taken from you? Which of these rights is most important to you? List them below. Why are they important? Write your reasons in a convincing and logical argument. Be prepared to defend your opinion in a class debate.

_____

_____

_____

_____

_____

_____

_____

_____

JEWS ENJOY THEIR NEW RIGHTS

Even before the addition of the Bill of Rights, the Jews were happy with their rights under the Constitution and wanted to show their appreciation of, and loyalty to, the new nation. On July 4, 1788, parades in many cities celebrated the **ratification** of the Constitution. The parades were planned to show the history of the nation and demonstrate its unity. Jews were among about 5,000 participants in the Grand Federal Procession in Philadelphia. The parade was a mile-and-a-half long and lasted three hours. Afterward, however, the Jews ate kosher food at a separate table.

Ratification means "formal approval."

Bigotry is intolerance of someone else's race, religion, beliefs, or practices.

What was important about the Jews' participation in this event and the table with kosher food? Can you think of other times when Jews attempted to integrate themselves into American society while also keeping their distinctive group identity?

During the next two years, several Jewish congregations exchanged letters with President Washington. The first Jewish community to write to the president was the Hebrew Congregation of Savannah, Georgia. On behalf of the congregation, Levi Sheftall thanked Washington for having "expelled that cloud of **bigotry** and superstition which has long . . . shaded religion" and for helping the Jews achieve "all the privileges . . . of free citizens." Washington, in reply, thanked the congregation, saying, "May the same wonder-working Deity, who has long since delivered the Hebrews from their Egyptian oppressors, planted them in the promised land . . . still continue to water them with the dews of heaven."

The big parade

Naphtali Phillips marched in the parade in Philadelphia when he was fifteen years old. Eighty years later, he described the experience in a letter to a friend:

My dear friend McAllister:

First, in an open carriage drawn by elegant horses, sat Chief Justice McKane [Thomas McKean] with other judges of the [Pennsylvania] Supreme Court, holding in his hand the new Constitution in a frame. This was received . . . with great rejoicing. . . . Then came farmers with large cattle and sheep on a platform drawn by horses all handsomely decorated. The farmers were sowing grain as they walked along. Then came an handsome ship elegantly adorned with flags . . ., manned by young mid-shipmen and drawn by horses, on wheels, and . . . they passed along singing out in true sailors' voice.

Next, a printing press on a platform drawn by horses, compositors setting types; and the press worked by journeymen distributing some printed matter as they went along. . . .

Next came blacksmiths with their forge, with a large bellows keeping up a blast to keep alive the flame of liberty. Next came shoemakers on a platform, men and boys soleing and heeltapping, others making wax ends. Then followed three fine-looking men dressed in black velvet, with large wigs on, densely powdered, representing the hairdressing society. Then the various trades followed with their appropriate insignia; young lads from different schools lead by their ministers and teachers, of which I was one of the boys.

The procession then proceeded . . . towards Bush Hill where there was a number of long tables loaded with all kinds of provisions, with a separate table for the Jews who could not partake of the meats from the other tables; but they had a full supply of soused [pickled] salmon, bread and crackers, almonds, raisins, etc. This table was under the charge of an old cobbler named Isaac Moses, well known in Philadelphia at that time. . . ."

from *American Jewish Archives* **(Jan. 1955)**

After much planning, the president of Mikveh Israel in Philadelphia wrote to President Washington on behalf of the Hebrew Congregations of Philadelphia, New York, Charleston, and Richmond, Virginia. The letter praised Washington and stated, "We acknowledge you, the Leader of American Armies, as his [God's] chosen and beloved servant." Washington replied that "The affection of such a people is a treasure. . . . May the same . . . eternal blessings which you implore for me, rest upon your congregations."

On August 17, 1790, Washington visited Newport. There, Moses Seixas of Congregation Jeshuat Israel presented him with a letter that expressed both the Jewish community's affection for him personally and its loyalty to the new nation. It also reminded Washington of past restrictions on Jews' rights and expressed their hope for full freedom under the new government.

This prayer composed and delivered by Reverend Gershom Mendes Seixas in 1784 calls on God to protect George Washington and Governor George Clinton.

The Jewish community and George Washington exchange letters

Moses Seixas for the Hebrew Congregation of Newport:

Permit the children of the stock of Abraham to approach you with the most cordial affection and esteem for your person and merit. . . .

*Deprived as we . . . have been of the invaluable rights of free citizens, we now—with a deep sense of gratitude to the Almighty . . . behold a government erected by the majesty of the people—a government which to bigotry gives no **sanction**, to persecution no assistance. . . ."*

George Washington's response:

While I received with much satisfaction your address . . . with expressions of esteem, I rejoice in the opportunity of assuring you that I shall always retain grateful remembrance of the cordial welcome I experienced on my visit to Newport. . . . The citizens of the United States of America have a right to applaud themselves for giving to Mankind examples of . . . a policy worthy of imitation. . . . Happily the Government of the United States, which gives to bigotry no sanction, to persecution no assistance, requires only that they who live under its protection should demean themselves as good citizens. . . .

May the children of the Stock of Abraham, who dwell in this land, continue to merit and enjoy the good will of the other Inhabitants; while every one shall sit under his own vine and fig tree, and there shall be none to make him afraid. . . .

These letters were published in several American newspapers in 1790 and were included in *A Collection of Speeches of the President of the United States* **(Boston, 1796).**

Sanction means "permission or approval of an authority."

THINK ABOUT IT These words of Washington—"the government of the United States, which gives to bigotry no sanction, to persecution no assistance"—have become famous. Note that they first appeared in Moses Seixas's letter to Washington. In your opinion, why were these letters—and their publication—important to the Jews in America in the 1790s?

DIFFERENT STATES, DIFFERENT RIGHTS

Even though the new government guaranteed the Jews religious freedom, not every state in the new Union did so. At first, most states did not give Jews full equality. Even though guarantees of religious freedom were written into every state's constitution, in some states only Protestants had full rights. In fact, Jews had different rights in different states. And to make matters more difficult, Jews were not an organized political force able to work together for change.

Create a seal

Here is a design that Benjamin Franklin, John Adams, and Thomas Jefferson proposed for the official seal of the United States at the Continental Congress in 1776. One side shows the splitting of the Red Sea (the Sea of Reeds) and the escape of the children of Israel from the Egyptian army. The story of the Exodus was an inspiration to those fighting for freedom. In the space below, create your own seal for the United States. Use a biblical theme if you wish. When you are satisfied with your design, copy it onto poster board, and display it in class.

Do It

George Washington's words that "everyone shall sit under his own vine and fig tree" come from a famous verse in the Book of Micah 4:3-4, "And they shall beat their swords into plowshares and their spears into pruning hooks. Nation shall not take up sword against nation; They shall never again know war; But every man shall sit under his grapevine or fig tree with no one to disturb him." Read these verses in a Tanach (Bible). Learn the song "Lo yisa goy el goy ḥerev" (Nation shall not take up sword against nation). Why, do you think, Washington used these words from the Bible? Write your own letter to Washington, explaining how you as a Jew feel about the new Constitution.

New York was the first state to give religious freedom to practitioners of every religion except Catholicism. In 1777, the state permitted the "free exercise and enjoyment of religious profession and worship" for everyone—but residents born in other countries were required to take an anti-Catholic oath. New York's Jews were the first American Jews to enjoy full citizenship—although after the War of 1812 some leading citizens of the state set out to convert its Jewish citizens.

In Philadelphia in 1784, Gershom Seixas and other Jewish leaders asked Pennsylvania to drop from its constitution a requirement that citizens acknowledge both "the Old and new Testament to be given by divine inspiration." (It is the same request that Jonas Phillips would make three years later to the delegates to the Constitutional Convention.) The request was set aside, but those words were removed from the state's 1790 constitution.

In the New England states and in New Jersey, Maryland, and North and South Carolina, state constitutions required men who sought public office to be Protestant. South Carolina's first constitution supported its requirement with

Do It

Lo yisa goy el goy ḥerev

Below are the words to this famous song in transliterated Hebrew and in English. If you play an instrument, you might want to find the music and learn to play it.

Lo yisa goy el goy ḥerev
Lo yil'm'du od mil-ḥamah

"Nation shall not lift up sword against nation
And they shall no longer learn the ways of war."

What do the words of this song mean to you, given what is happening in the world today?

_____

_____

_____

_____

_____

ישעיהו פרק ב פסוק ד

לא ישא גוי אל גוי חרב ולא ילמדו עד מלחמה.

a quotation from the Anglican Book of Common Prayer. In 1797, Solomon Etting and Bernard Gratz petitioned the Maryland legislature, requesting that Jews "be placed on the same footing as other good citizens." The request was called "reasonable," but the bill it spawned—which became known as the Jew bill—was not passed for almost thirty years. Etting then became one of the first Jews elected to office in Maryland—he was elected to Baltimore's city council and later became its president.

In North Carolina, a Jewish state legislator named Jacob Henry almost lost his office in 1809 because of his religion. It was discovered that Henry had not taken a required oath upholding Christianity. It was decided, however, that Jews could hold **legislative office**—but not **civil office.** Jews in North Carolina did not receive full political equality until 1868.

A **legislative office** is one involved in making law.

A **civil office** is concerned with running the government.

In the early 1800s, Rhode Island and Connecticut still had charters written in the 1660s. The Revolution had not improved the status of Jews there. In 1820, Thomas Jefferson wrote to Jacob De La Motta, a Jewish physician in Charleston, that he was delighted to see that American Jews had full social rights and hoped that "they will be seen taking their seats on the benches of science as preparatory to their doing the same at the board of government." By 1830, most states had granted Jews equal rights, although New Hampshire's Jews had to wait until 1877.

THINK ABOUT IT

What is your reaction to the differences in laws from state to state?

America's founders were aware of the Jews' difficult history, and they were responsive to their needs. The Jewish people gained important rights in the new nation.

CLICK ON IT

The Freedom Forum Online website covers First Amendment issues. See www.freedomforum.org.

The struggles of a Jew in American politics

Benjamin Nones fought for the patriots during the Revolution and returned to Philadelphia after the war. He was active in politics, in an antislavery society, and in synagogue and charitable activities. Like many other Jews, Nones was a Jeffersonian Republican and was attacked by the Federalists as a Jew. After he attended a Republican convention in Philadelphia, the city's major Federalist newspaper, the *Gazette*, published an attack on him as "a Jew, a Republican, and poor." Nones responded with his own piece in the *Aurora*, a Jeffersonian newspaper, in which he expressed his pride in his Jewish identity and the Republican cause. He wrote, "I am a Jew, and if for no other reason, for that reason am I a republican. . . . In republics we have rights, in monarchies we live but to experience wrongs. . . . How then can a Jew but be a Republican."

DO IT

Find out about your own state's constitution. What does it say about freedom of religion?

Find out what you can about First Amendment issues today. These include posting the Ten Commandments on public buildings, wearing religious symbols or articles of clothing, offering prayers at public events, and using school buildings for meetings sponsored by religious groups.

Themes: ① Jewish integration into secular community
② Women getting rights.

CHAPTER 6
CHANGES IN JEWS AND JUDAISM

What important changes affected the Jewish community in America in the late 1700s and early 1800s?

The new nation began to grow and change, and so did its Jewish community. Between 1790 and 1820, the population of the United States grew from 3.9 million to 9.6 million. The Jewish population during that time grew from 1,500 to 2,700. New ideas about freedom and equality affected the Jewish community—sometimes in unexpected ways.

CHANGES IN DAILY LIFE

After the Revolution, many Jews left Philadelphia, where they had gone to escape the British troops, and either returned to their homes or settled elsewhere. Charleston soon had the largest Jewish community, whereas most of Newport's Jews did not return. As Jews left the large cities and settled in small towns, about half of the Jewish men found jobs in business. Some, like Jacob Franks of Wisconsin, were fur traders. Others became merchants, brokers, auctioneers, and shopkeepers. Some were involved in stock exchanges or in the transportation industry. The Gratz family, among others, made a fortune in land **speculation.** In 1776, they bought land in western Virginia and in the upper Ohio basin. In 1784, Daniel Boone surveyed territory for the Gratz family in the area that would become Kentucky.

Katrina

Speculation is a business situation in which a person takes a big risk in the hope of making a large gain.

Jews found new opportunities in the secular community. For example, Brown University began to admit Jewish students. When Columbia College required that a representative of every major religion serve on its board of directors, Gershom Seixas, *hazan* of Shearith Israel, became a trustee. Humane societies, trade societies, and similar organizations began accepting Jews as members.

The Gold and Silversmiths' Society of New York elected Myer Myers as its president. Myers' silver bowls, trays, and candlesticks had gained respect and admiration in the secular community, as had his ritual objects in the Jewish community.

What do you think the Jews of that time felt as America opened up to them? Do you think that there were negative aspects of the changes as well as positive aspects? Why?

JEWS MAKE THEIR MARK

Many of the foremost American Jews of the early nineteenth century succeeded in integrating their Judaism with their secular lives. One, Mordecai Manuel Noah, was the editor of several New York City newspapers, and served as a Democratic politician, a lawyer, a judge, a diplomat, a surveyor for the port of New York, and sheriff of New York County. He also wrote plays about freedom and spoke out in defense of New York's Jews when they were attacked. The city's Jews chose him to be president of the Hebrew Benevolent Society.

In 1813, President James Madison appointed him consul to Tunis—a dangerous job. Americans were being held hostage there, and Noah, working through an agent, managed to free some of them. He was supposed to handle the matter secretly, but he did not. In addition, he had not been authorized to hire the agent, and he paid the man more money than his budget allowed. Noah had expected to be hailed as a hero. Instead, he was dismissed. He was told that the government had not realized that his Judaism would be an obstacle to his service in a Muslim country. That was an excuse, however; in fact, Madison had not wanted anyone to publicize this only partially successful mission. Foreign diplomats, American politicians, and Jewish citizens spoke out in support of Noah, but he lost the position anyway.

What challenges do Jews working for the United States in foreign countries, or in other government positions, face today? Is their Judaism ever an issue?

The Touro brothers (sons of the *hazan* Isaac Touro) were also successful in both the Jewish and the secular worlds. One son, Abraham, made his home in New Orleans, which became part of the United States in 1803, as a result of the Louisiana Purchase. The city was a major port, and he built a large shipping business there. He then moved to Boston and set up a successful shipyard in nearby New Bedford. When he died, he left a great deal of money to charities, some of which were Jewish and some of which were not.

His brother, Judah, also found success in New Orleans. He began with a small store and became a wealthy merchant and trader. During the War of 1812, he enlisted in the military. He was wounded in the last battle of the war, the battle of New Orleans, and left to die. A friend— a Christian—came back for him and got him to a hospital in time to save his life.

Even though he was not a frequent participant in synagogue services, Judah, like his brother, was known for contributing to a variety of charities, including the synagogue in New Orleans. He also set up the city's first public library and its first public infirmary, the Touro Clinic. And he donated $10,000 to build the Bunker Hill Monument in Charlestown, near Boston.

Just before his death, Judah Touro wrote his will. Known as the "will of the century," it named as heirs sixty individuals and organizations, both Jewish and non-Jewish. These included eight orphanages, twenty-two "Hebrew congregations" from New York to Saint Louis, Missouri, two hospitals, and an almshouse for the aged and the poor of New Orleans. He gave special gifts for Jewish education

in New York, Philadelphia, and New Orleans. And because he was concerned about the Jews of Palestine, he left $60,000 to their community. He asked Sir Moses Montefiore, an English **philanthropist,** to decide how to spend the money. Montefiore used it to build rows of stone houses in the Yemin Moshe quarter of Jerusalem.

Another Jew who combined his Judaism with his secular American life was Uriah Phillips Levy. Levy was a fifth-generation American and a first cousin of Mordecai Manuel Noah. At the age of ten, he ran away from his home in Philadelphia to become a ship's cabin boy. He came home in time to prepare for his bar mitzvah but returned to the sea when he was fourteen. By the time he

A **philanthropist** is a person who is charitable.

Touro remembered

Judah Touro is buried in Newport, Rhode Island. His tombstone says:

"The last of his name, he inscribed it in the Book of Philanthropy, to be remembered forever."

What would you want to be remembered for? Do you think it is important for Jews to give to non-Jewish, as well as Jewish, causes? Why or why not?

DO IT

On a map of Jerusalem, find the street named for Judah Touro.

was twenty, he was the captain of a merchant ship. Levy served in the U.S. Navy during the War of 1812. After his ship was captured, he spent time as a prisoner of war in England. During his time in the navy, he was court-martialed six times. He claimed that his treatment was a consequence of religious prejudice. Despite the discrimination, Levy worked his way through the ranks and was made captain of the warship *Vandalia*. He instituted a new approach to discipline by banning the punishment of **flogging**, and he supported a bill in Congress that outlawed flogging in America's navy.

 Flogging is the punishment of publicly whipping a person.

Later, Levy took command of the *Macedonian* in the Mediterranean Sea. As commodore of the Mediterranean Squadron, he was the first Jew to hold so high a rank in the U.S. Navy. He also wrote the navy's official handbook, *Manual of Rules and Regulations for Men-of-War* which promoted his vision of a modern navy.

Levy and Monticello

In 1836, Levy bought Thomas Jefferson's former home in Virginia, Monticello, in order to preserve it. Levy's elderly mother, Rachel, spent her last years there, and her grave is on the grounds. When he died, Levy left the property to the "People of the United States" as an agricultural school for the orphaned children of navy officers. A great deal was to happen before the Thomas Jefferson Memorial Fund would take possession of the property in 1923.

Levy defends himself

Once Levy was charged with being unfit to serve as an officer. In his defense he wrote,

*My parents were Israelites, and I was nurtured in the faith of my ancestors. In deciding to **adhere** to it, I have but exercised a right guaranteed to me by the Constitution of my native state and of the United States . . . I have never failed to respect the like freedom of others. . . .*

*From the time it became known to the officers of my age and grade that I aspired to a lieutenancy, I was forced to encounter a large share of the prejudices and hostility by which, for so many ages, the Jew has been pursued. I ask you to unite with the wisest and best men of our own country and of Europe in denouncing these sentiments, not only as injurious to the peace and welfare of the community, but as repugnant to every **dictate** of reason, humanity, and justice."*

Levy won his case and was reinstated.

DO IT Find out about the Levy family's eighty-seven-year ownership of Monticello.

 To **adhere** to something means "to stay with it."

A **dictate** is a principle.

 CLICK ON IT Check the website www.monticello.org. Go to "About Us" and then "Related Links: The Levys at Monticello."

CHANGES IN SYNAGOGUE LIFE

After the Revolution, many congregations were reestablished, and a number of new synagogues were built in Richmond, Savannah, Charleston, and Philadelphia. Influenced by the spirit of the Revolution and the new Republic, Jews became less willing to accept a synagogue in which only the wealthier and more socially important members made the decisions for everyone. Many synagogues changed their constitutions, doing away with policies that seemed undemocratic. The new constitutions spoke of freedom and equality, just as the U.S. and state constitutions did.

There were other democratic innovations. Special seating for prominent families was eliminated, all members began to vote in yearly elections of synagogue officers, and members gained the right to change and approve their congregations' constitutions and bylaws. Shearith Israel's new constitution eliminated differences in the treatment of members and nonmembers and made it easier for any member to hold office in the government of the synagogue. Following a change that Jews saw in Christian churches, Beth Shalome in Richmond invited—rather than required—all Jews in the community to become members.

 THINK ABOUT IT What impact might the new, voluntary nature of synagogue participation have had? We take this kind of participation for granted today.

Synagogues' constitutions

Synagogues first used the term constitution soon after America's constitution came into being. Before then, the governing documents of synagogues were usually called *haskamot*. Several congregations in the eighteenth century tried to fine members for violating the Sabbath, not attending Shabbat services, eating nonkosher food, and similar violations of Jewish law. Members found to be in violation of the regulations would be excluded from synagogue honors and banned from serving on the board of trustees. Some congregations forbade Jews who had intermarried to become members or participate in religious ceremonies. Most of those rules could not be enforced, however, and were later changed or abolished.

A declaration of synagogue rights (1790)

The Declaration of Synagogue Rights was written by the members of Congregation Shearith Israel in New York City after the Revolution. The language shows how much impact the fight for freedom had on the Jews of the country.

 LOOK AT IT

Whereas in free states all power originates and is derived from the people, who always retain every right necessary for their well being individually. . . . In like manner the individuals of every society in such state are entitled to and retain their several rights, which ought to be preserved inviolate.

Therefore we . . . conceive it our duty to make this declaration of our rights and privileges:

First, of Jews in general. That every free person professing the Jewish religion, and who lives according to its holy precepts, is entitled to worship the god of Israel in the synagogue, and by purchase or gift to have a seat therein, and to be treated in all respect as a brother, and as such a subject of every fraternal duty.

Secondly. Of those who have been for a length of time members . . . though not reputed yehidim [members]: That all these who have formerly and now continue to be members of this kahal kodosh [holy congregation] at large, not having subscribed to the constitutions of the aforesaid congregation, but living as worthy professors of our holy law, are entitled to the several privileges in the foregoing articles, and shall be called to sepher [reading of the Scroll] when not interfering with the [prior] rights of a yahid. . . .

Ninthly. In all general meetings . . . or any other usual meetings, every yahid has and ought to have a right of debating on any subject whatsoever with decency, yet to deliver his sentiments without restraint, and freely to give his opinions and advice concerning any matters in question, or to open a new subject in order, at his own option. . . ."

DO IT Find out about your synagogue's constitution, or bylaws. Who may join? Who may be elected to office? Do you agree with these laws? What changes would you make? Compare these bylaws to the Declaration of Synagogue Rights (above). Write your own bylaws for a synagogue in which you would like to be a member.

Synagogues imitated other practices of Christian churches: some held lotteries to raise money; some began to use the secular calendar rather than the Jewish calendar in their congregational records. Feeling more accepted by the larger community, Jews sometimes invited non-Jewish community leaders to participate in synagogue dedications. Jews also asked members of other religions to help repay synagogue debts, and some Jews donated money to Christian causes. When Congregation Mikveh Israel in Philadelphia made a public request for money to pay its debts, Benjamin Franklin was one of the first to volunteer to help.

In religious services, the blessing that had been recited for the British royal family was replaced by a prayer for national and state leaders. Members of Shearith Israel no longer stood for the government blessing. And when Gershom Seixas returned to New York, he recited in English instead of Portuguese the names of government officials to be blessed.

During this time, Americans in general were becoming less religious, and for Jews the idea of a community completely organized around the synagogue began to change. In New York, Jews demanded the right to choose their own *shohet,* a job that had once been controlled by the synagogue. Other organizations, such as the Female Hebrew **Benevolent** Society in Philadelphia, were beginning to develop and would become important to the community.

In addition, Ashkenazic Jews began to establish separate synagogues. For some time, newly arriving Ashkenazic Jews had become members of synagogues that followed Sephardic rituals. Eventually, some Ashkenazic Jews felt the need to assert their separateness. In 1795, German Jewish immigrants broke away from Mikveh

Israel in Philadelphia to establish the German Hebrew Society, which later became Rodeph Sholom. In 1825, German congregants in New York broke from Shearith Israel to establish B'nai Jeshurun. This process was repeated in other cities. Later, there were other divisions. In 1828 in New York, a group of Polish Jews left B'nai Jeshurun to found Anshe Chesed, which had an eastern-European style.

Between 1776 and about 1840, some Jews became less strict in their religious practices. Almost one-third of Jews intermarried. Nonetheless, other Jews were struggling to preserve their traditions and institutions. For example, Rebecca Samuel and her family left Petersburg, Virginia, for Charleston so that they could join a more established Jewish community, where she could educate her children in Judaism and live an observant Jewish life.

THINK ABOUT IT What is your opinion of the changes in American Jewish religious and daily life?

WOMEN MAKE CHANGES IN JEWISH LIFE

In both Protestant churches and the Jewish community, women were becoming more active in religious life. One woman who encouraged Jews to help one another and pay more attention to their religion was Rebecca Gratz. The daughter of Michael Gratz, who helped develop Indiana, Illinois, and Kentucky, Rebecca was a member of a wealthy Philadelphia family. She was well-known for her work both inside and outside the Jewish community, for her interest in helping people, and for her excellent organizational skills. By the time she was twenty, Gratz was the secretary of the Female Association for the Relief of Women and Children in Reduced Circumstances, the first **nonsectarian** group in Philadelphia to help the poor. In 1819, she helped found the Female Hebrew Benevolent Society, the first American Jewish women's group, the first Jewish charity in America outside a synagogue, and the first organization to serve the poor of the Jewish community. It provided food, clothing, shelter, and an employment bureau.

DO IT

In your synagogue's siddur [prayer book], find the blessing for the country. What does it say? When does your congregation recite it? Does the congregation stand? How do you feel about reciting it? Discuss this blessing with your rabbi.

LEARN IT **Benevolent** means kind, caring, compassionate, and desiring to do good for others.

Nonsectarian means not part of any specific religious group.

A letter to Newport

DO IT

LOOK AT IT

Some congregations in the United States moved away from traditional Jewish practices. Remember that many of the early settlers were descended from the Conversos of Spain and Portugal, who had not been permitted to practice their religion. The letter on this page is from Manuel Josephson of Philadelphia to Moses Seixas. What can you learn from the letter about the practices of Jews of the eighteenth century?

_____

_____

_____

_____

_____

_____

from Publications of the American Jewish Historical Society 27 (1920)

Philadelphia, 4th February 1790

Mr. Moses Seixas
Dear Sir,

On the 22d. of Decemr. last I was favoured with your obliging Letter. . . . You insinuate that to . . . alter your present Mode would be very impracticable or at best attended with much difficulty . . . having been adopted not from choice but necessity: nevertheless, if ye were convinced that what I advanced . . . was the result of Mature deliberation ye would one & all subscribe to my opinion; . . . I shall therefore endeavour to convince you that what I wrote is literally just & comformable to our Oral Law as deduced & digested from Scripture, and by no means matter of Opinion of my own. . . . But the case in question is distinctly to be found in all our Law books of the first reputation . . .

You say Mr. Rivera reads Hebrew perfectly, surely then it can't be so mighty a task for him to read from the Sefer [Torah] a few chapters occasionally; . . . I . . . have no doubt that, on his being made acquainted with the preceding passages which shew that reading the Parasah [portion] from the Sefer [Torah] is essential & strictly commanded by our Laws, . . . he will not hesitate to perform that part of the service. . .; or if that should not be agreeable to read the words although without the Ta'amim [chanting] would still be preferable to your present mode. . . .

I duly observe what you are pleased to say respecting the blowing of Shofar [ram's horn], your reasons for not performing that solemn & strictly enjoined service are beyond doubt of great weight; for there is no Din [ruling] to be found that insists on blowing a Shofar where there is none. . . . By your letter it appears that you have instructed Mr. David Lopez Junr. to procure you one at Hamburg. . . . In the interim . . . I doubt not you might procure the Loan of one from New York. . . .

Dr. Sir yr esteemed friend & hum. Ser.
Manuel Josephson

Rebecca Gratz was always concerned with Jewish children and their religious education. In 1838, she began the Hebrew Sunday School Society. It followed the model of the Christian Sunday school and was the first Jewish school of its kind in the country. At first, the classes used Christian Bible translations and hymnbooks, since there were no Jewish books in English for children, but in places the text had to be changed. The school became a model for Jewish education in America. It was open to children from the entire Philadelphia Jewish community without a fee. Rebecca Gratz was the school's superintendent until 1864.

Although as a young woman she attended many dances and parties, Rebecca Gratz never married. She made a home for her unmarried brothers and raised the nine children of her sister, Rachel, who died in 1823. When she died, in 1869, she was considered one of the most important Jewish women in America.

Another Jewish woman who made a difference in the life of her community was Penina Moise. Moise was born in Charleston in 1797 to French Jewish parents who were refugees from a slave revolt in the West Indies. When her father died, she had to leave school, but she continued to study by herself. She became the superintendent of the Sunday school of Charleston's Congregation Beth Elohim, and eventually she and her sister started a girls' school. She also wrote poetry for newspapers and magazines. Her favorite work was writing hymns based on the Psalms. They were collected in the first Jewish book of hymns printed in English in America. In 1833, Moise published *Fancy's Sketch Book,* a collection of her poems. It was unusual for several reasons: It was the first published book of poetry by an American Jewish woman; it was published under her own name instead of a **pseudonym;** and it dealt with political issues. Moise's poems also expressed her feelings about the rights of Jews around the world.

 A **pseudonym** is a name someone uses to hide his or her identity.

 In your opinion, why did conditions in America lead to women's increased involvement in religious life?

AN ADDITIONAL CHALLENGE

Despite their newly acquired rights, Jews still faced Christian efforts to convert them. A group of Protestant ministers formed the American Society for **Meliorating** the Condition of the Jews. The organization used its publication, *Israel's Advocate,* to argue for conversion. A man named Solomon Henry Jackson used his own journal, *The Jew,* to criticize this interference in Jewish life. Jackson voiced contempt for Jews who converted. He also declared that the Protestant organization's true goal was not to convert Jews, but to stir up hatred of Jews and spread antisemitism. The fact that Jackson could write so openly demonstrated the strength of the Jews' rights in America. By 1825, Jackson announced that he would cease publication of his journal because, he said, Christian publications had become more liberal.

 Meliorating is a form of **ameliorate,** which means "to make better."

 What would you do if you were approached by a person or group that wanted to persuade you to convert to Christianity?

Jews were taking active roles in American society, and American society was leaving its mark on American Judaism. Independence, so cherished by Americans, had become an important aspect of American Jewish life, inside and outside the synagogue. Voluntarism and individualism, other key values of American life, also became aspects of American Jewish life.

 Why was it important for Jews to make their mark in America by combining their American and Jewish identities? Can you think of people today who have accomplished something similar?

Rebecca Gratz and the heroine of *Ivanhoe*

Over the years, it has been said that Rebecca Gratz was the model for Sir Walter Scott's character Rebecca in his novel *Ivanhoe*, which was published in 1820. In the novel, Rebecca, a Jew, says, "Among our people have been women who gave their thoughts to heaven and their actions to works of kindness. . . . Among these will Rebecca be numbered." Although these words do describe the life and work of Rebecca Gratz, modern historians have found no proof that Scott was inspired by Gratz.

Penina Moise's hymns and poems

Penina Moise wrote poems and hymns about Judaism. When a new building for Beth Elohim was dedicated, the first hymn of the service was one written by Moise. Read the section of that hymn below. What do you think of Moise's poetry?

*Hear, O Supreme! Our humble **invocation:** Our country, kindred, and the stranger bless! Bless too, this sanctuary's **consecration,** Its hallowed purpose on our hearts impress.*

Still, still, let choral harmony
Ascend before Thy Throne;
While echoing Seraphim reply:
The Lord our God is One!

An **invocation** is a prayer.

Consecration means "dedication."

Can you write a poem of your own that you might like to include in a service at your synagogue?

_____

_____

_____

_____

_____

_____

Word find

Some important terms from Unit 2 are hidden in this puzzle. See If you can find the following words and names:

Constitution
amendment
Seixas
Hays
Washington
Etting
Tories
Whigs
Salomon
Patriot
revolution
Noah
Touro
Levy
Gratz
Moise

```
W  R  E  G  U  I  Z  R  A  F  X  U  M  O
L  S  E  I  X  A  S  N  O  M  O  L  A  S
C  E  B  T  U  O  L  U  K  N  H  E  M  O
K  I  V  E  N  O  I  T  U  L  O  V  E  R
F  R  G  Y  O  M  O  P  E  W  Q  S  N  U
B  O  U  J  T  O  I  R  T  A  P  C  D  O
Z  T  A  R  G  B  R  E  H  I  P  O  M  T
H  M  O  K  N  E  W  K  N  T  E  F  E  V
H  A  Y  S  I  M  O  I  S  E  T  B  N  W
C  E  O  R  H  E  W  G  S  Q  T  F  T  M
Z  C  O  N  S  T  I  T  U  T  I  O  N  E
V  E  F  T  A  H  Y  O  I  P  N  N  U  J
Y  U  O  K  W  K  E  T  S  W  G  V  R  S
Q  E  Y  R  E  X  E  H  I  P  K  L  N  R
```

UNIT 2 TIME LINE OF HISTORICAL EVENTS:
THE REVOLUTIONARY WAR AND THE NEW REPUBLIC

1765	1770	1775	1780	1785	1790	1795	1800

AMERICA

1768: Citizens of Boston refuse to quarter British troops.

1783: Great Britain recognizes U.S. independence.

1788: New York becomes capital of the United States.

1772: Boston Assembly demands colonies' rights and threatens to secede from Great Britain.

1789: Washington is inaugurated as first president of the United States.

1775: George Washington becomes commander-in-chief of the American army.

1790: Philadelphia becomes capital of the United States; Washington, D.C., is founded.

JEWISH AMERICA

1773: First published Jewish sermon, preached in Newport, is printed in America.

1794: Charleston Jewish community dedicates Beth Elohim.

1777: New York State's constitution grants freedom of religion.

1795: Philadelphia's Jewish community establishes the first Ashkenazic synagogue in America (later named Rodeph Shalom).

1782: Philadelphia's Mikveh Israel is formally organized, its building is dedicated, and its governing document is called a constitution.

1786: Aaron Levy announces plans to build Aaronsburg, the first town in America to be named for a Jew. The plan is unsuccessful.

1789: Gershom Seixas attends George Washington's inauguration.

JEWISH WORLD

1781: Joseph II of Austria rescinds law requiring Jews to wear distinctive badges; Sir William Frederick Hershel discovers the planet Uranus.

1791: France grants Jews privileges of full citizens; tsarist Russia confines Jews to Pale of Settlement.

1783: Moses Mendelssohn completes translation of the Pentateuch into German using Hebrew letters.

1799: Napoleon's army moves from Egypt, captures Haifa, and advances to Akko before being stopped.

1784: Louis XVI of France abolishes tax on Jews to enter certain cities; in Austria, first Jewish public school opens combining Jewish and secular subjects.

1788: First convicts, including six Jews, arrive in Australia. John Harris, a Jew, when freed, becomes first policeman in Australia.

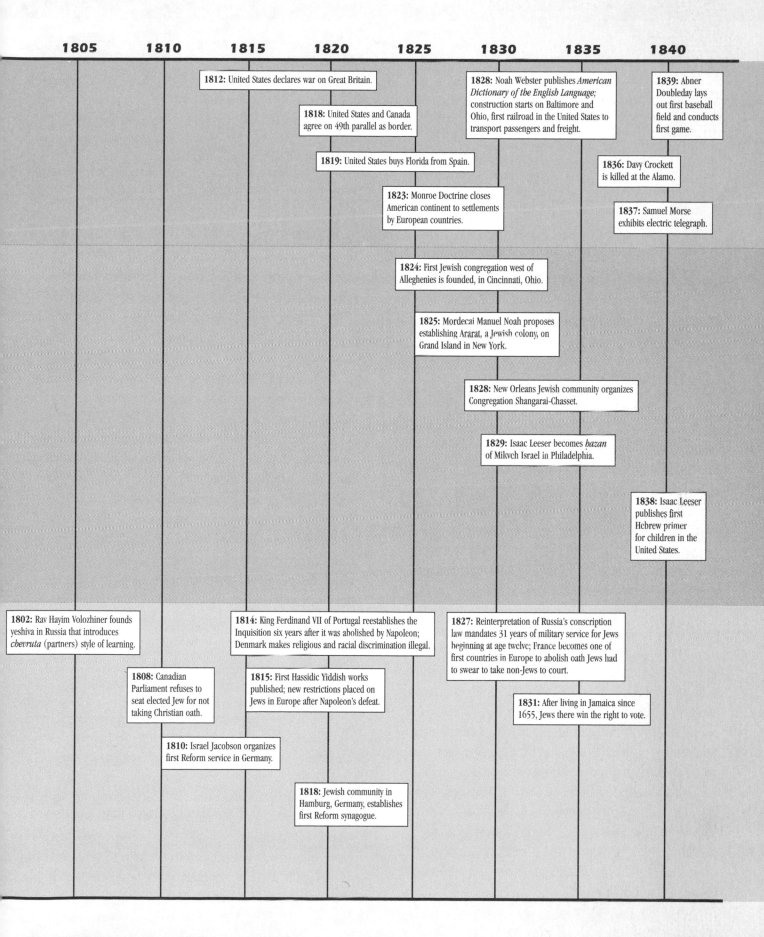

1805 **1810** **1815** **1820** **1825** **1830** **1835** **1840**

1812: United States declares war on Great Britain.

1828: Noah Webster publishes *American Dictionary of the English Language;* construction starts on Baltimore and Ohio, first railroad in the United States to transport passengers and freight.

1839: Abner Doubleday lays out first baseball field and conducts first game.

1818: United States and Canada agree on 49th parallel as border.

1819: United States buys Florida from Spain.

1836: Davy Crockett is killed at the Alamo.

1823: Monroe Doctrine closes American continent to settlements by European countries.

1837: Samuel Morse exhibits electric telegraph.

1824: First Jewish congregation west of Alleghenies is founded, in Cincinnati, Ohio.

1825: Mordecai Manuel Noah proposes establishing Ararat, a Jewish colony, on Grand Island in New York.

1828: New Orleans Jewish community organizes Congregation Shangarai-Chasset.

1829: Isaac Leeser becomes *ḥazan* of Mikvch Israel in Philadelphia.

1838: Isaac Leeser publishes first Hebrew primer for children in the United States.

1802: Rav Hayim Volozhiner founds yeshiva in Russia that introduces *chevruta* (partners) style of learning.

1814: King Ferdinand VII of Portugal reestablishes the Inquisition six years after it was abolished by Napoleon; Denmark makes religious and racial discrimination illegal.

1827: Reinterpretation of Russia's conscription law mandates 31 years of military service for Jews beginning at age twelve; France becomes one of first countries in Europe to abolish oath Jews had to swear to take non-Jews to court.

1808: Canadian Parliament refuses to seat elected Jew for not taking Christian oath.

1815: First Hassidic Yiddish works published; new restrictions placed on Jews in Europe after Napoleon's defeat.

1831: After living in Jamaica since 1655, Jews there win the right to vote.

1810: Israel Jacobson organizes first Reform service in Germany.

1818: Jewish community in Hamburg, Germany, establishes first Reform synagogue.

CHAPTER 7
BECOMING AMERICANS

[handwritten annotation: • Jews were discriminated against • Not everybody could get to America]

What contributions did central European Jews make to the American economy and society?
What impact did the new immigrants have on Jewish community life in the United States?

Jews had come to America from the earliest colonial days. But the first big wave of Jewish immigrants arrived in the 1830s. Already, most of the nation's 10,000 to 15,000 Jews were Ashkenazim. Now, their brothers and sisters from Germany and other central and eastern European countries—such as Poland, Austria, and Hungary—joined them. A trickle became a flood. By 1880, there were between 230,000 and 300,000 Jews in America. Most were determined to become Americans.

BACK IN EUROPE

There were many reasons that Jews, as well as non-Jews, chose to leave central Europe in the nineteenth century. Along with their non-Jewish neighbors, Jews encountered difficulties adjusting to the changes brought about by the Industrial Revolution. Many crafts became obsolete. Many people lost jobs. About half of the Jews were living below the poverty line.

In addition, there were strong anti-Jewish feelings. Jews in many areas suffered the loss of their civil rights. Violent anti-Jewish riots had rocked central Europe in 1819; and there were other riots in connection with the revolution of 1848. In the German states, laws barred Jews from some trades and professions unless they had letters of "protection." In the state of Bavaria, in southern Germany, in order "not to enlarge the number of Jewish families in places where they already exist," laws limited the rights of Jews' to settle and to marry. A Jewish man who wanted to marry had to buy an expensive certificate, called a *matrikel,* proving that he was in a "respectable" trade or profession. Usually only the firstborn son could obtain a *matrikel.* Jews often had to pay especially heavy taxes as well, and some faced discrimination by gentile craftsmen. Making matters worse, one German newspaper wrote that killing a Jew should be treated as a misdemeanor rather than a serious crime.

America had great appeal; it was a land of opportunity. The idea of going to America grew in popularity as Jews who had made the trip wrote to family and friends at home. There were plenty of opportunities for anyone who was willing to work. German Jewish newspapers discussed the idea. One paper asked, "Why should not young Jews transfer their desires and powers to hospitable North America, where they can live freely alongside members of all confessions . . . [and] where they don't at least have to bear this?" Jews were eager to go to a place where they would be seen as compatriots, not as outsiders. During the nineteenth century, some German communities lost as much as 70 percent of their Jews.

THINK ABOUT IT
How would you feel about leaving your home—even one where you faced prejudice and discrimination—to live in a new country?

At first, most of the immigrants were the poorer Jews from small towns and villages. Most were artisans. They could not afford to move their families to America. Individual family members traveled to America alone, and once they had earned enough money, they would send for other family members. Usually, it was young, single men who came, but some young, single women came in the early years as well. After 1848, a small number of better-educated Jews from the larger cities arrived.

The Jews' journey from the old country

Circle the places mentioned in Unit 3 on this map of Europe:

Bavaria, Germany

Amsterdam, The Netherlands

Cadiz, Spain

London, England

Poland

Austria

Hungary

from Samuel Rawson Gardiner, ed., *Gardiner's Atlas of English History* (London: Longmans, Green, and Co. 1914)

The trip to America was very hard. First, immigrants traveled across Europe by coach, or wagon or on foot to reach port cities. They carried with them dried kosher food, family Bibles, and prayer books. Then, they faced the difficult voyage across the Atlantic, by sail.

One journey to America

In a letter to his family in 1819, Wolf Samuel wrote,

I left Amsterdam on September 13th with 96 passengers, including 6 Jews. First of all we entered the North Sea where I was seasick for four days. I thought I was going to die. Then we had a very bad wind for a whole month and no prospect of getting to America. We hadn't much food left and the water was foul, and the . . . captain put into the harbor [in Falmouth] in England. . . . We stayed there ten days. We put out to sea and again we met a great storm and we all thought that we were going down. The stores ran out a second time and the captain had to run for shore and we arrived in Cadiz in Spain, where none of us Jews was allowed in the town as our lives would not have been safe. We lay in Cadiz for 14 days. Then we left Cadiz and put out into the Atlantic Ocean and with a good wind arrived at Baltimore in 62 or 63 days, that is . . . after a voyage of 5 months."

from Howard M. Sachar, *A History of the Jews in America* (New York: Vintage Books, 1993)

Find out who in your family came to America from another country. If possible, interview them to find out what the experience was like. How did they get here? What kind of jobs did they find? Where did they live? Tape-record or videotape the interviews.

LIFE IN AMERICA

While most of the new Jewish immigrants tended to live in cities—such as New York, Philadelphia, Saint Louis, Cincinnati, Baltimore, New Orleans, and San Francisco—others lived in smaller towns and even outlying areas. They played an important part in America's growing economy, especially in manufacturing and sales. While a few of them became bankers and department-store owners, most had more modest success.

Many of the immigrants were **itinerant** peddlers, and some set up shops. Peddlers filled their packs with anything and everything they could carry. Peddling did not require an outlay of much money, only enough to buy a license. Things to sell—such as dishes, sewing supplies, and tools—could be bought on credit from Jews who had arrived in the country earlier. Quite a few immigrants sold secondhand clothing. Others worked as artisans, especially as glaziers, cigar makers, and tailors. Women usually worked as shopkeepers, seamstresses, boardinghouse managers, and teachers. Some of the new arrivals remained very poor and received financial assistance from Jewish charitable organizations.

Itinerant means "wandering" or "traveling."

In time, Jewish immigrants became manufacturers of various goods, including clothing and shoes. They were especially important in the production and sale of ready-made clothing. This was a field that had grown in the mid-nineteenth century because of the invention of the sewing machine—by Elias Howe in about 1846—and the demand for uniforms during the Civil War. In New York by 1880, Jews owned about 80 percent of all retail and 90 percent of all wholesale clothing firms. Outside New York, about 75 percent of clothing firms were Jewish owned. The Chicago company, Hart, Schaffner and Marx, would become the largest manufacturer of men's clothing in the world.

Joseph Seligman and Marcus Goldman were among the Jewish immigrants who arrived with very little money, worked as peddlers, and became wealthy businessmen, financiers, and bankers. They joined a small but influential group of community leaders and philanthropists, some of whom later played key roles in the American government. Joseph Seligman had a close relationship with President Ulysses S. Grant. Two sons of the immigrant Lazarus Straus (who with his sons, became the owner of Macy's department store) also had illustrious careers. Isidor Straus was a U.S. congressman and was offered, but did not accept, the Democratic nomination for mayor of New York City. His brother Oscar was U.S. Ambassador to Constantinople, and as the secretary of commerce and labor under President Theodore Roosevelt, became the first Jew to serve in the cabinet.

 THINK ABOUT IT Why was the business success of these Jewish immigrants important to the future of the American Jewish community?

Most of the new immigrants were traditional Jews. In America, however, observance was not easy. Jewish communities were small and scattered, and Jews remained a tiny minority. Sometimes the need to earn a living made the observance of Shabbat and Jewish holidays difficult. And the American emphasis on individuality encouraged some immigrants to throw off their traditions. For others, the choice was difficult. One man wrote in his diary, "God of Israel, thou knowest my thoughts. Thou alone knowest my grief when on the Sabbath's eve, I must retire [alone] to my lodging and on Saturday morning carry my pack on my back, **profaning** the holy day, God's gift to His people of Israel."

 LEARN IT **Profaning** means "treating disrespectfully."

A peddler's journal

 **DO IT** In 1842, twenty-three-year-old Abraham Kohn of Fürth, in Germany, set out from New York for Massachusetts. There were few Jews in New England—the first congregation in Connecticut was not formed until 1840, and the Newport Jewish community had virtually disappeared after the Revolution. The first religious services in Massachusetts were held in 1842, the first Jewish community in Maine was begun in the late 1840s, and there was no Jewish community in Vermont or New Hampshire until after the Civil War. Life was difficult for Kohn. On the right are some sections of his journal.

Write a journal entry of your own, telling what it is like for you to be a Jewish peddler traveling through America, trying to make your living.

_____

_____

_____

_____

_____

from Kenneth Libo and Irving Howe, _We Lived There Too: In Their Own Words and Pictures—Pioneer Jews and the Westward Movement, 1630–1930_ **(New York: St. Martin's/Marek, 1984)**

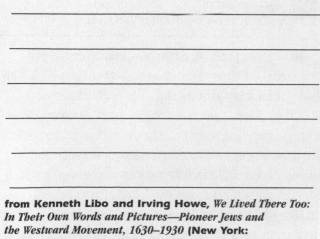 **LOOK AT IT** Is it liberty when, in order to do business in a single state, one has to buy a license for $100 and profane the holy Sabbath, observing Sunday instead? True, one does not bear the name "Jew," but only because one does not utter it. Can a man, in fact, be said to be "living" as he plods through the vast, remote country, uncertain even as to which farmer will provide him shelter for the coming night? O, that I had never seen this land, but had remained in Germany, apprenticed to a humble country craftsman!

As far as the language is concerned, I am getting along pretty well. But the Americans are a peculiar people. Although they sit together by the dozen in taverns, they turn their backs to each other. No one talks to anybody else. Is this customary of a republic? I don't like it. Is this the fashion of the nineteenth century? I don't like it either.

How much more I could write about this queer land. It likes comfort extremely. The Germans, by comparison, hardly know the meaning of the word. The wife of an American farmer—for hours she can sit in her rocking chair shaking back and forth as she thinks of nothing but beautiful clothes and a fine hairdo. The farmer himself is able to sit down for a few hours every day to read his paper and smoke his cigar.

The whole country looks to me like an adolescent youth. That is America! Although she appears to know everything, her knowledge is, in truth, very elementary. American history is composed of Independence and Washington—that is all.

Find out which activities, according to halachah, are and are not permitted on Shabbat. What is the reason for these prohibitions?

In most places where Jews settled, if there were at least ten Jewish men over the age of thirteen, a prayer group was formed. When the Jews in an area collected enough money, they hired a leader. This person, who was not an ordained rabbi, filled many roles in the Jewish community. He acted as a religious leader and preacher. He circumcised baby boys, read Torah, blew the shofar, and collected members' dues. Most of these men knew a little bit of Hebrew, and they needed the work. Sometimes, however, they were reprimanded for not displaying behavior befitting a rabbi.

THINK ABOUT IT What do you think the most difficult part of being a new Jewish immigrant in America would have been?

ONE JEWISH LEADER

One of the most outstanding Jewish leaders of the time was Isaac Leeser, of Philadelphia's Sephardic Mikveh Israel synagogue. Leeser attended high school in Europe, studied Hebrew grammar, and had some knowledge of the Talmud.

When he arrived in the United States in 1824, he worked in his uncle's general store in Richmond and served as an assistant to the *hazan*. Even though he was Ashkenazic, he mastered Sephardic rituals in a few weeks. He learned to read and write English in

two years. Because of the reputation he earned in Richmond, he was invited to serve as the *hazan* of Mikveh Israel in 1829.

Many Jews who arrived from central Europe enrolled their children in public schools. The newer immigrants found those schools unsatisfactory, however, and in the 1840s there was an increase in Jewish day schools. Leeser believed that Jewish children needed an education rooted in Judaism, and he favored day schools. He was also practical, however, and he supported Rebecca Gratz's Hebrew Sunday School Society in Philadelphia, a school that students attended only one day a week. Since there were few textbooks for Jewish children, Leeser began to publish them.

His first book, in 1830, was a translation of *Instruction in the Mosaic Religion,* a textbook for children published by a teacher in Germany. In 1835, Leeser published *Catechism for Younger Children* and, three years later, *The Hebrew Reader.* He prepared the *Reader,* a first book of lessons in Hebrew, for Rebecca Gratz's Sunday school. Gratz wrote of Leeser, "with his strangely pock-marked face, golden spectacles and inexhaustible fund of ever-ready information, he knew every child and teacher, called each by name, and nothing was too trivial or intricate to claim his clear explanation."

LEARN IT A **catechism** is a summary of the principles of a religion in the form of questions and answers. Catechisms were used for educational purposes, mostly in Christian religious schools. Some Jews adapted the format in their own schools.

THINK ABOUT IT Why was it important for Jews in America to establish Jewish schools—either day schools or "Sunday" schools?

In order to promote day-school education, Leeser organized the Hebrew Education Society of Philadelphia in 1846. The society provided for "the establishment of a school or schools within . . . Philadelphia, in which are to be taught the elementary branches of education, together with the sciences, and modern and ancient languages, always in combination with instruction in Hebrew language, literature and religion." In 1867, Leeser also helped establish Maimonides College, the first rabbinical seminary in America. (It closed in 1873.)

Although he was traditional in his observance of Judaism, Leeser wanted to unite Jews across the United States. He was open to change and gave religious services an American touch by using some English and delivering sermons. He traveled around the country, visiting many congregations. He was well-known for his speeches and his writing and published ten volumes of sermons.

Leeser produced English and Hebrew versions of both Sephardic and Ashkenazic prayer books, as well as an English translation of the Bible. His was the first such translation in America by a Jew. In 1843, he began editing the first successful English-language Jewish magazine, *The Occident.* He used the magazine to unite Jews and to promote Jewish literary achievements in English. He made sure that each issue included poetry and fiction by Jewish writers. In his magazine, Leeser also defended Jews against the efforts of Christian missionaries. In one article, "The United States Not a Christian State," published in 1850, he wrote that America was not Christian by law, even though most Americans were Christians.

In 1845, Leeser organized the Jewish Publication Society, which published fourteen volumes of works by Jews, including Leeser's own book, *The Jews and Their Religion,* before a fire, in 1851, destroyed all its books and put it out of business. (Another Jewish publication society was established in 1871, and a third, which still exists, in 1888.)

Catechism for Jewish children

Designed as a Religious Manual for House and School by Isaac Leeser

Below are the first four questions and answers from Chapter VI: ("The Moral Law") of Leeser's book.

What does the moral law teach?

It teaches us our duty.

What is this duty?

We must do whatever God demands of us.

What obliges us to do this?

By the possession of the life given by God we are from motives of gratitude compelled to obey his wishes; and by the benefits which He daily and hourly bestows on us, we should be induced to show that we are not unworthy of his fatherly care; and lastly, as children of the covenant with the Lord, it is reasonable that we should repay his especial kindness by a more ardent display of activity in the fulfillment of our duties.

Towards whom have we duties to perform?

Towards God, through whose favour we live.

Towards our fellow-men, who, as well as ourselves, have received life and being from God.

Towards ourselves, both as regards our body and our soul.

(Philadelphia: L. Johnson, 1863)

You can read more of Leeser's catechism online at www.jewish-history.com in the "Virtual Library."

Choose a Jewish topic that you know well—or one that you want to know more about and can do some research on. Write your own catechism about it below. Try to write at least three questions and answers.

Question 1: _____

Answer 1: _____

Question 2: _____

Answer 2: _____

Question 3: _____

Answer 3: _____

"Not A Christian state"

Leeser wrote:

We have often maintained, both in private conversation and in our writings, that no one can claim for the United States the name of a Christian state, in the legal sense of the words; which does not say that the whole people of the country might not, for all that, be Christians. . . . The proposition, we always thought, was so evident, that we could not help wondering, and our astonishment is not lessened at this day, that people should even dare to call this a Christian country, and speak of the population as a Christian people. . . . The laws of the country . . . leave every man to pursue whatever religion he pleases. . . . All men have an equal right to be here; one does not tolerate the other, nor has he to thank him, legally, for leaving him undisturbed, however practically the minority are at the mercy of the majority. Might makes right here as well as elsewhere; and the fanatics for all opinions know this perfectly well, and they therefore endeavour to make their views those of the majority, that they may carry them through and force them on the community by the brute power of numbers.

from Jonathan D. Sarna and David G. Dalin, *Religion and State in the American Jewish Experience* **(Notre Dame, Ind.: University of Notre Dame Press, 1997)**

What is your reaction to Leeser's article? Do you agree that America is not a Christian country legally? practically? Do you agree that members of the majority religion sometimes try to force their opinions on others? Has this ever happened to you? What do you do, or would you do, when this happens?

Find out about the Jewish charitable, social, educational, recreational, and other organizations in your community. Do you, your parents, or your friends belong to any of them? Why belong to a Jewish organization, rather than a secular one?

THE JEWISH COMMUNITY SPREADS

Jewish community life was developing in the United States in the nineteenth century. Many philanthropic, social, cultural, recreational, and educational institutions were being formed. Benevolent societies provided needy Jewish families with food, fuel, loans, shelter, care for the sick, and burial. In many communities, Jewish orphanages served the neediest families. By 1860 in New York City alone, there were forty-four charitable organizations. Jews' Hospital (now Mount Sinai Hospital) began as a shelter serving kosher food. Over time, it added medicines and other modern services. Jews in Philadelphia also wanted to help one another. The city had seventeen charitable and **fraternal** groups. In many towns, such organizations met the immigrants' social, cultural, and economic needs. Many charitable groups were supported by membership dues and fund-raising events, such as charity balls.

Fraternal has to do with a society of men.

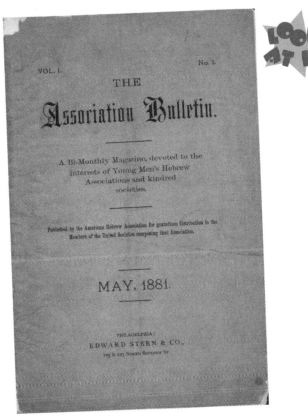

LOOK AT IT

A cover from a magazine for YMHA members.

Jewish literary societies also began around this time. The first were founded in the 1840s for men only, but women soon started their own groups. Several Jewish publications, such as Leeser's *Occident,* Isaac Mayer Wise's *American Israelite* and *The Deborah,* and Samuel Myer Isaacs' *Jewish Messenger* were founded. The immigrants produced novels and poetry that focused on Jewish and American themes. And for the first time in the United States, traditional Jewish scholarship began to develop. **Haggadot,** prayer books, Bibles, and Bible translations, educational materials, and collections of sermons were published.

In the 1850s, clubs for young Jews in America began using the name Young Men's Hebrew Association (YMHA). The name was adapted from the Young Men's Christian Association (YMCA). But while the YMCA's activities were mostly religious and athletic, the YMHA's program included literary groups, classes, athletics, lectures, orchestras, glee clubs, libraries, drama, debates on topics of Jewish interest, and sometimes, employment bureaus.

Haggadot (Haggadahs) are books that contain the story and prayers read at the Passover seder.

Another big effort to help Jews band together throughout the country was an organization called B'nai B'rith ("Children of the Covenant"). It began in New York in 1843 to reach out to Jews, some of whom did not belong to synagogues, giving them an opportunity to spend time with people who shared their ethnic and cultural heritage. Using the motto "Benevolence, Brotherly Love, and Harmony," B'nai B'rith did not stress religious practice but emphasized the ties that bind Jews together even if they disagree about matters of faith. It was modeled after the general—not specifically Jewish—lodges of the day, and some of B'nai B'rith's founders were members of those groups.

Although there were a number of other Jewish lodges, B'nai B'rith was the best known. It provided its members with social activities, as well as sick and burial benefits. It also supported educational programs, charitable institutions (such as orphanages), and protested against discrimination against Jews both in the United States and abroad. B'nai B'rith was so successful in bringing together Jews of all backgrounds and religious beliefs that by 1861 it had branches in every major American Jewish community, and by 1890 national membership had reached 30,000. The organization even started branches in Europe.

Find out what B'nai B'rith does today. Also learn about the work of the Anti-Defamation League (ADL, founded in 1913 and now an independent organization) and Hillel, an organization of students on college campuses, first established at the University of Illinois in 1925. (Hillel has been independent since 1988.) Visit or call the Hillel office at a college near your home.

Go online to Hillel's national website at www.hillel.org.

JEWS SPEAK OUT

As they built new community institutions and developed their cultural life, American Jews felt a greater sense of unity. Christians who got to know their Jewish neighbors generally treated them fairly. And when Jews were not treated fairly, they realized that they could speak out. They could become involved in issues of religion and state and forcefully meet any challenges to Jewish rights.

In 1840, American Jews organized themselves, for the first time, in order to protest the Damascus affair. That name refers to a false accusation by the French consul in Damascus, Syria. The consul claimed that in a religious ritual, Jews had murdered a Capuchin monk, Brother Thomas, who indeed had disappeared. Many Jews were arrested, and more than sixty Jewish children were taken by the Syrian authorities in order to make their parents "confess."

The French and English Jewish communities sent delegations to Damascus to protest. Led by Isaac Leeser and others, American Jews organized protests in many cities, requesting that President Martin Van Buren intervene in the case. The president instructed American diplomats in Constantinople and Alexandria, Egypt, to express American outrage at the blood **libel**. In addition, Secretary of State John Forsyth wrote to the Syrian authorities, protesting the persecution. The combined European and American efforts were finally successful in obtaining the release of the prisoners, as well as an official decree from the sultan acknowledging that the charges were false.

 A **libel** is a false, damaging statement about someone.

 Why was the Damascus affair important to the Jewish community in America and around the world? Are there situations today that you think the American or world Jewish communities should speak out about?

John Forsyth steps up

Secretary of State John Forsyth wrote to John Gliddon, the U.S. consul at Alexandria and instructed him to intercede for the Jews of Damascus. This letter was written on August 14, 1840:

In common with all civilized nations, the people of the United States have learned with horror, the atrocious crimes imputed to the Jews of Damascus, and the cruelties of which they have been the victims. The President fully participates in the public feeling, and he cannot refrain from expressing equal surprise and pain, that in this advanced age, such unnatural practices should be ascribed to any portion of the religious world, and such barbarous measure be resorted to, in order to compel the confession of . . . guilt; the offenses with which these unfortunate people are charged, resemble too much those which, in less enlightened times, were made the pretexts of fanatical persecution . . . to permit a doubt that they are equally unfounded.

from Jacob Rader Marcus, ed., *The Jew in the American World: A Source Book* (Detroit: Wayne State University Press, 1996)

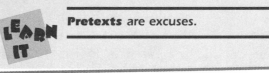 **Pretexts** are excuses.

In another infamous incident, the Mortara affair of 1858, an Italian Jewish boy was secretly baptized by his nurse and later kidnapped, to be raised in the Catholic Church. Once again, American Jews organized protest rallies in many cities. This time the president, James Buchanan, was not willing to get involved. However, the affair led to the organization of the Board of Delegates of American Israelites in 1859. The Board, which was intended to unify American Jews, had cultural, educational, charitable, and religious functions. It was mainly a defense organization, however, protecting Jewish rights in the United States and abroad. Even though it was not entirely successful in achieving its goal, the organization's existence was important. It became part of the Union of American Hebrew Congregations in 1878.

In 1850, the United States and the Swiss Confederation had signed a treaty that stated, "Christians alone are entitled to the enjoyment of the privileges guaranteed by the present Article in the Swiss Cantons." This meant that American Jews could be denied entry permits and commercial privileges that American Christians had in Switzerland. (In some cantons, native Jewish residents were also denied civil rights.) This provision became known in 1857, when a visiting American Jewish businessman, A. H. Gottman, was asked to leave the canton of Neuchâtel because of his religion. American Jews objected strongly and spoke out against the treaty. They pointed out that the American government did not allow religion to be a consideration in granting political and economic rights in the United States, and therefore should not permit such a provision in agreements with other countries.

President Buchanan asked Secretary of State Lewis Cass to express American objections. In the end, the expulsion order against Gottman was rescinded, and the Swiss constitution was amended to guarantee equality to all citizens and foreign visitors regardless of their religion.

Should the United States get involved in political or religious events in other countries? Why or why not?

The Swiss Treaty

Part of a protest by American Jews against the Swiss Treaty says,

As citizens of the United States, we can not but consider such a construction antagonistic to the progressive, liberal policy of our government, and unworthy of the . . . fame which that policy has achieved; and as Israelites, we must feel mortified, should our government sanction Switzerland's slander upon religion.

from Jonathan D. Sarna and David G. Dalin, *Religion and State in the American Jewish Experience* **(Notre Dame, Ind.: University of Notre Dame Press, 1997)**

A LASTING INFLUENCE

The immigration of Jews from central European countries to the United States had greatly increased the number of Jews in America. It also had a lasting influence on their cultural, political, and social lives. The community grew, and grew stronger, thanks to the contributions of this remarkable group of immigrants.

Is there one event, person, or contribution that you think had the greatest effect on the lives of Jews in America in the nineteenth century? What is it, and why?

Jewish immigrants about to enter the United States through Galveston, Texas.

CHAPTER 8
WESTWARD, HO!

What were some of the ways in which Jews took part in the migration to the great American West?

Despite what some people think, not all the central European Jewish immigrants to the United States settled in New York or other East Coast cities. Some of the more adventurous followed the other hardy Americans and non-Jewish immigrants who headed west to seek their fortune in the wide-open land from the Mississippi Valley to the Pacific Ocean. There was a need for settlers on the frontier, and since many of the Jewish immigrants were peddlers traveling with their wares, the frontier offered great opportunities. Westward, ho!

WHERE THEY WENT AND HOW THEY GOT THERE

Some of the Jewish immigrants from Europe arrived in the port of New Orleans—and stayed. They made New Orleans a center of Jewish life in the South. Others continued up the Mississippi River. They made their homes in the cotton-market town of Memphis, Tennessee, or in mill towns like Natchez and Vicksburg, Mississippi, and Shreveport, Louisiana. Some found work in Baton Rouge, Louisiana, a cotton-shipping town. At least a few Jewish families settled in almost every important southern town.

A small number of Jewish merchants settled in Texas in the 1820s and 1830s and in New Mexico in the 1840s, when those two future states were part of Mexico. One of those settlers, Adolphus Sterne, smuggled arms to Sam Houston, then fought for the independence of Texas from Mexican rule. When the Republic of Texas was established in 1836, every man who was the head of a family was granted 1,200 acres of land, and single men received 640 acres. Five years later, a law was passed that allowed Sam Houston, the president of Texas, to grant larger parcels of land. Henri Castro, a wealthy French Jew, was allowed to start a colony, called Castroville, in Southwest Texas. With his own money, Castro brought 485 families and 457 single men, including some with Jewish names,

from France and Germany. Buildings were started and crops were planted. Although Castro eventually lost his fortune, he continued to lead the little town until his death, in 1861.

Other Jewish immigrants landed at ports in eastern cities, peddled for a while, and moved on when they heard about opportunities in the West. They traveled on the Erie Canal, which had opened in 1825, to Buffalo, New York. From there, they went further inland. Some settled in Cleveland, Cincinnati, and Saint Louis, which all became important centers of Jewish life. Others made their way to the Ohio River, where they boarded boats headed west. Some reached California by sailing to Panama or Nicaragua, traveling by land across Central America to the Pacific Ocean, and boarding ships sailing north. And some traveled west the traditional way—by wagon train.

How would you feel about being one of the only Jews in a very small frontier town? How large is your Jewish community? What are the advantages and disadvantages of a large—or small—Jewish community?

Jews move west

On this map of the United States since 1855, circle the places listed below.

Louisiana	Missouri	New Mexico
Tennessee	Texas	Colorado
Mississippi	Nebraska	Oklahoma
New York	California	Nevada
Ohio	Maryland	Utah

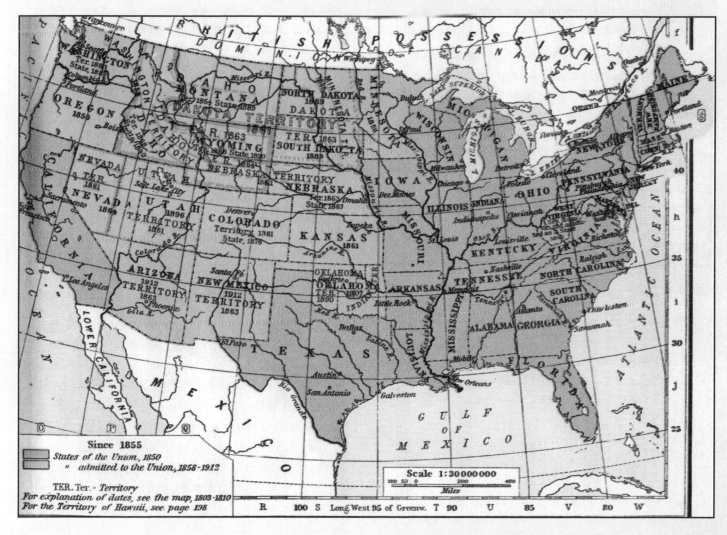

Getting there the hard way

A young immigrant named Adolph Sutro, who went west in 1850 during the gold rush, took the difficult and dangerous route across Central America. Colonel John C. Frémont, a military hero and future presidential candidate, joined Sutro and two women in a one-hundred-dollar canoe ride sixty-five miles down the alligator-filled waters of the Chagres River to Cruces, Panama. There, Sutro bought a mule to carry him the rest of the way to Panama City and a second mule to carry bales of cotton for his future business.

One day, he fainted while riding. When he awoke, both of his mules and eight of his bales of cotton were gone. He walked the ten remaining miles to Panama City, carrying two bales of cotton and dragging two. There, he spent a week with little food while he tried to find passage on a ship to San Francisco. Because he could not afford to ship all four bales of cotton, he left two behind. Onboard the ship, people were dying of yellow fever. By the time Sutro reached California, the gold rush was over.

WHAT THEY DID

Jews who headed west found communities that were as open and free as the land. There were many opportunities to make a fortune and few restrictions. Non-Jews saw them simply as fellow pioneers. In this new land, Jews often assumed positions of leadership. Many were active in local government, serving on juries, school boards, city councils, and state legislatures; some even served as mayors. Single men who found ways to make money often returned east to find wives. Their communities followed a pattern: The men created congregations, cemeteries, and charitable societies. The women started their own charitable groups. Hospitals, schools, and other organizations soon followed.

About 200 Jews headed to Omaha, Nebraska, a city that grew as a trading center after gold was discovered at Pikes Peak, Colorado, in 1858, and silver and lead were found elsewhere in the Rocky Mountains. Many of those Jews found great success trading with Indian tribes. A man named Julius Meyer, who lived for weeks at a time with the Pawnees, was elected an honorary chief. He was called Box-ka-re-sha-has-ta-ka, "Curly-Headed White Chief with One Tongue."

Other Jews, however, fought the Indians. Sigmund Schlesinger, who was born in Hungary, came to New York and kept going west. On the Kansas frontier, he served as an Indian scout. Once his company was attacked by a band of Cheyennes and Sioux, and the siege lasted four days.

From a frontier journal

In his journal, Schlesinger wrote, "About 12 Indians marched on us. Stampeedet 7 Horses. 10 Minuts after, about 600 Indians attacket us. . . . Wounded 19 Man & Killt all the Horses. We was without Grubb & Water all day. Dug Holes in the sand whith our Hands." The next day, he continued: "In the night I dug my hole deeper, cut of meat oof of the Horses & hung it up on Bushes. Indians made a charge on us at Day brake but retreated. Kept Shooting nearly all day. They Put up a White flag. Left us at 9 o'clock in the evening. Raind all night." He ended with "Scalpt 3 Indians which were found about 15 Feet from my hole consealt in Grass. . . . Killt a Coyote & eat him all up."

from Kenneth Libo and Irving Howe, *We Lived There Too: In Their Own Words and Pictures—Pioneer Jews and the Westward Movement, 1630–1930* (New York: St. Martin's/Marek, 1984)

A few Jews became **prospectors** in the Rockies, but most worked in business, running general stores, saloons, and hotels. Others moved to the Southwest and worked as peddlers and traders among Oklahoma's Creek Indians. They bought buffalo hides, wolf pelts, **tallow,** and feathers and shipped them to Saint Louis. One of these Jewish peddlers was Henry Mayer, who left Germany in 1834 at age seventeen and went to New Orleans. He started peddling on the Santa Fe Trail, expanding his company with profits from each trip he took to Chihuahua, Mexico. When he married, he took his wife, Rebecca, to Chihuahua on their honeymoon, with 500 mules and fifty men. Eventually, they settled in San Antonio, Texas, where they sponsored holiday services and a religious school for the new Jewish community there.

Prospectors explore an area looking for precious metals.

Tallow is the hard fat from the carcasses of sheep or cows that is used to make candles and soap.

A letter home

Pioneers kept journals and wrote letters to family and friends back home. Read this letter from an immigrant in California to his brother. Then write a letter in the space below to your family after your trip to your new home in the West.

_____

_____

_____

_____

_____

_____

_____

_____

_____

_____

San Francisco, Calif., Jan. 13, 1854

Dear Brother,

It was a wonderful surprise to learn from a fellow named Liwey [Levy?] that you are in America! And also that you are living in Baltimore with a family named Herzog. . . .

How are you getting along and how's business? It's not great here since as you can imagine things don't just fall in your lap. Here I have learned what business means, and I have put up with a lot, especially in Panama. I was sick there for several months and had no money, not even enough to eat. As I got a little better I got various jobs to pay for board and room, which cost a dollar-and-a-half a day. I was too weak even to play my guitar.

But with God's help I got well, and after 4–5 months in Panama in that awful year I was able to put away 120 dollars in gold which I earned in just 5 weeks. Then I was able to go to California! . . .

I have now been in California seven months, in San Francisco, and am married! I have a fine wife and thank God things are going quite well. I have already taken in several hundred dollars. If you would want to come here then you and I and my wife would start up a nice café with music and singing every evening. Here a cigar costs 1 or 2 schillings each, and drinks the same, so there is money to be made. Also I am as well known in San Francisco as I was in Cologne. . . .

Regards from my wife who is looking forward to meeting you.

Your brother, J. Felsenthal

from Jacob Rader Marcus, ed., *The Jew in the American World: A Source Book* (Detroit: Wayne State University Press, 1996)

THINK ABOUT IT

How did the life of a pioneer change those Jews who moved west?

Why were Jews generally well-accepted in frontier towns?

EUREKA! GOLD IS DISCOVERED

San Francisco was a most welcoming home to America's Jews. After gold was discovered at Sutter's Mill in 1849, more than 40,000 prospectors rushed to the area seeking their fortune. About 300 Jews joined the California gold rush. Those who did not find gold made a living as peddlers and traders, selling supplies to the gold and silver prospectors. Some became store owners or manufacturers, especially of clothing. Jews were well-accepted in San Francisco, and quite a few joined the city's economic elite. One of the most successful was Levi Strauss, who manufactured the heavy denim pants called Levis.

Levi's Levis

Levi Strauss, who gave his name to that most American item of clothing—blue jeans—was born Loeb Strauss in Bavaria in 1829. Two years after his father died, Loeb and his mother and sisters went to New York. They were met by his older brothers, Jonas and Louis, who had started a **dry-goods** business, J. Strauss Brother & Co. Loeb began to learn the business. By 1850, his family and friends were calling him Levi.

LEVI STRAUSS COPPER RIVETED OVERALLS

LEVI'S ELECTRIC RODEO — THE TALK OF TREASURE ISLAND

When he learned of the California gold rush, Levi went to San Francisco to make his fortune. He decided to sell supplies to the miners who arrived in the city to outfit themselves before heading off to the gold fields. He arrived in San Francisco in 1853 and started a dry-goods business under his own name, in addition to serving as the West Coast representative of the family business.

As the company continued to grow, it moved to increasingly larger buildings, and in 1863 it was renamed Levi Strauss & Co. Strauss was well-known around the city. He was also active in the Jewish community and was a member of San Francisco's Temple Emanu-El ("God Is With Us"). He contributed to several Jewish charities and to the gold medal that was given each year to the synagogue's best Sabbath-school student.

A tailor named Jacob Davis of Reno, Nevada, had a customer who kept ripping the pockets of any pants Davis made for him. Davis, a customer of Strauss & Co., wanted to strengthen the pants, so he put metal rivets where the pants often tore, such as at the pocket corners and at the bottom of the button fly.

The pants were a big success, and Davis wanted to be sure that no one stole his idea, but he did not have the $68 legal fee that was needed to apply for a patent. He knew he needed a

business partner, and he thought of Levi Strauss. On May 20, 1873, the two men received patent 139,121—and blue jeans were born. Holding the patent meant that for almost twenty years, Levi Strauss & Co. was the only company permitted to make and sell clothing with rivets.

At first, the firm manufactured waist overalls (the old name for jeans) by giving the material to women who did the sewing in their homes. Jacob Davis was in charge of manufacturing, and demand was soon so great that the company opened two factories. In 1890, the year that the number 501 was used for the overalls for the first time, Levi and his nephews, who were working with him, officially incorporated the company.

Despite his importance in the business community, Strauss insisted that his employees call him Levi, not Mr. Strauss. He was well-known for his generosity to both Jewish and non-Jewish causes. When Levi Strauss died in 1902, he was remembered in the *San Francisco Call* for his "fairness and integrity . . . with his customers and liberality toward his employees."

Dry goods are fabrics and items such as thread, needles, buttons, and so on.

BUILDING A JEWISH LIFE

Even in the middle of the rush for gold, Jewish pioneers did not forget their Judaism. A Yom Kippur service was held in a tent in San Francisco in 1849, and Congregation Sherith Israel was organized that same year. Because the congregation had no building of its own, it held services in a variety of places, several of which were destroyed by fire. In 1852, the congregation bought property on Stockton Street and raised funds to build a synagogue. The brick-fronted one-hundred-foot-long building was finished in one month.

The congregation was strictly Orthodox and followed the Polish *minhag.* Until 1857, it had no regular leader, so the *mohel* or the *shohet* led the religious services. Then H. A. Henry was appointed rabbi. Henry was extremely well respected and remained the congregation's rabbi for many years.

Minhag means "custom" or "tradition."

A **mohel** is someone who performs circumcisions according to Jewish ritual.

In 1854, the synagogue of a second congregation was dedicated. Congregation Emanu-El was bigger than Sherith Israel and followed the German tradition. After many changes in leadership, the congregation hired Dr. Elkan Cohn, who introduced Reform practices. Men and women sat together, a choir and organ were used during services, and religious poems in Hebrew were omitted from the service. The congregation was successful and was soon considering constructing a larger building.

As the Jewish community of San Francisco expanded, other organizations added life to the community. In 1857, for example, a Hebrew Young Men's Literary Association was meeting every other week to discuss politics, religion, history, and other topics of interest. A number of Jewish settlers also became active in civic affairs. By 1865, there were 4,000 Jews among the 119,000 residents of San Francisco.

If you were helping to start a new Jewish community in a town, what would you do first? Why? What must be in place in order for a Jewish community to exist and grow?

A western Haggadah

On the frontier, even the story of Pesaḥ was seen through a special lens. Fred Hard, a newspaper editor in the mining town of Austin, Nevada, wrote the following story. In 1864, when he wrote this, there were 150 "Israelites" living there, "including three families." Draw a few pictures to illustrate this western Haggadah.

When Pharaoh was Khedeve of Egypt, he was building government buildings by contract, and the Israelites were working for him making brick by the day. Like all government contractors, he neither furnished a good article nor treated his employees with justice.

The Israelites struck for higher wages and eight hours a day, and organized a trade union and elected a man named Moses as President. Moses was in the clothing business; and because he didn't know anything about labor the Israelites thought he would make a good presiding officer of a labor organization.

When the Israelites struck, Old Pharaoh hired a new set of hands, and the Israelites concluded to go on a prospecting trip into Canaan District, where there was represented to be a big milk and honey ledge. Owing to the snow blockade on the Suez Canal the market was bare of yeast powders, and the mill that made the self-rising flour had shut down; and as the Israelites were afraid the claims would all be located if they didn't get there quick, they started off with a few sacks of flour and mixed bread in the flour sack and baked it on a hot rock.

After they had crossed the creek Pharaoh missed some picks and shovels, and thinking the Israelites had stolen them, he swore out a search warrant and sent a sheriff's posse after them. The sheriff's party missed the ford and were drowned, and to this day the Israelites eat unleavened bread in commemoration of the event.

from Kenneth Libo and Irving Howe, *We Lived There Too: In Their Own Words and Pictures—Pioneer Jews and the Westward Movement, 1630–1930* **(New York: St. Martin's/Marek, 1984)**

THE MAYOR OF SAN FRANCISCO

Adolph Sutro—the man who traveled through Central America on his way to San Francisco—sold the bales of cotton he had brought from Panama and opened a small tobacco shop. Nine years later, when he got word of the discovery of silver in Nevada's Comstock lode, he decided to buy a mine in the Sierra Nevada Mountains. But by the time he sold his business and reached the mountains, all the shares in the mine had been sold. So instead of buying a mine, he set up a mill to process the silver. He soon learned that ventilation problems and flooding were plaguing the mine. Sutro figured out a way to correct the problems—by drilling a huge tunnel parallel to the mine. The Sutro Tunnel, which took ten years to complete, became a model for other mines. When it was complete, Sutro sold his interest in the venture and returned to San Francisco as a real estate developer.

Sutro bought thousands of acres of land in the city. A cottage overlooking the Pacific and much of the land around it became his private estate. He then began to share his good fortune. He bought a rundown house just below his and had it made it into a castle. He filled Cliff House with stuffed animals, totem poles, armor, coin collections, and even Egyptian mummies. Next to it he installed huge public swimming pools that were filled with heated ocean water. There were slides, ladders, and hanging rings to play on. The public was welcome to stroll through the gardens and enjoy its statues, gazebos, and topiary. And because Sutro thought that the ten-cent streetcar fare was too expensive, he built his own railroad line and charged only five cents for the ride from the city.

Sutro was elected mayor of San Francisco in 1894. He did not have any political connections, however, and was not interested in making any. After one term, he returned to his estate and continued his good works for the city. He donated land to expand the University of California at San Francisco, sponsored Arbor Day plantings to create Sutro Forest, and built one of the biggest private libraries, which he made available to the public. He also sponsored many events for children.

PIONEERS IN SOUTHERN CALIFORNIA

Other Jews headed for southern California. One, Solomon Nunes Carvalho, was the official artist and photographer for the Fremont expedition which explored large areas of the West. In 1853, Colonel John C. Frémont invited Carvalho to join his expedition to map the West. Frémont wanted to find a suitable route for a railroad across the Rocky Mountains and the Continental Divide.

Carvalho had taught himself to paint and then had learned the art of making **daguerreotypes.** His job on the Frémont expedition was to photograph the route the railroad would follow.

Daguerreotypes are photographic prints made on silvered copper plates. Named after their French inventor, Louis Daguerre, they are an early form of photography.

The expedition was difficult and dangerous. Carvalho's equipment was heavy, and with the extreme temperatures (sometimes as cold as thirty degrees below zero), the process of making one picture could take more than an hour. In December, the party began to run out of supplies. Carvalho had to leave his equipment behind. When their food supply ran out, the men slaughtered their horses and mules. At first, Carvalho refused to eat the unkosher meat. Soon, however, he realized that Jewish law required him to eat unkosher food rather than die.

Finally, in February 1854, the expedition reached the Mormon settlement of Parowan, Utah. Carvalho weighed less than one hundred pounds. The settlers nursed him and his companions back to health, and from Parowan, Carvalho traveled to Salt Lake City to meet Brigham Young, the Mormon leader. Young liked Carvalho, who, like him was a Bible scholar. He invited Carvalho to join him at a meeting with Walkara, chief of the Ute Indians. Carvalho sketched the two men as they talked about a way to settle the problems between their peoples.

Carvalho finally left Utah for Los Angeles, where he became one of the founders of that city's Jewish community. He helped start the first Jewish organization in the city, the Los Angeles Hebrew Benevolent Society. Soon, however, he returned to the wife and children he had left behind in Baltimore. There, he helped found a synagogue, Beth Israel, which was one of the first synagogues in America to include English prayers in its services.

While San Francisco had become a busy city, Los Angeles remained a small western town until after the Civil War. Only a few thousand settlers lived there—in a jumble of flat-roofed houses that spread out into the prairie.

One of those early settlers, Joseph Newmark, first immigrated to New York in 1824. From there, he moved to Connecticut, Missouri, and Iowa, starting synagogues along the way, before moving on to Los Angeles. In Los Angeles, he helped found the Hebrew Benevolent Society. Subsequent generations of his family expanded his business and had a religious and cultural effect on the community.

A JEWISH WOMAN AND A LAWMAN

In the Kansas Territory, Dodge City councilman Adolph Gluck hired a sharpshooter named Wyatt Earp to enforce the law. Earp had earlier met and married a young Jewish woman, Josephine Sarah Marcus. Josie Marcus had moved to San Francisco from New York with her parents who were German immigrants. After seeing a theater production of *H.M.S. Pinafore*, Marcus ran away with the theater company when it left town. She arrived in Tombstone, Arizona, and fell in love with the town's sheriff, Johnny Behan. Behan introduced her to Earp, a deputy U.S. marshal. Soon, Earp and Marcus fell in love and married.

Carvalho's adventure

Solomon Carvalho wrote a bestselling account of his expedition with Frémont, called *Incidents of Travel and Adventure in the Far West* (1856). In it, he wrote about one night on the trail:

One of my feet was badly frozen, and I walked with much pain and difficulty. . . . I was the last man on the trail, and my energy and firmness almost deserted me. Alone, disabled, with no possible assistance from mortal man, I felt my last hour had come . . . I [finally] came into camp about ten o'clock at night. It requires a personal experience to appreciate the intense mental suffering which I endured that night.

from Michael Feldberg, ed., *Blessings of Freedom: Chapters in American Jewish History* (New York: KTAV, 2001)

DO IT

Find out what Jewish law would say about Carvalho's dietary dilemma. A hint: Think about the principle of *pikuah nefesh*, "saving a life." Another hint: Rabbi Akiba said, "A person is not permitted to harm himself or herself" (Mishnah, *Bava Kamma* 8:6).

In 1881, U.S. Marshal Wyatt Earp, his brothers Virgil and Morgan, and their friend Doc Holliday, took part in the famed thirty-second shoot-out with their enemies, the Clanton gang, at the O.K. Corral. Three members of the gang were killed, and Virgil and Morgan Earp were wounded. Each side charged the other with shooting first. The Earps were acquitted in court, but the Clanton gang took revenge, killing Morgan Earp. In turn, Wyatt and Doc Holliday killed the men they thought had helped kill Morgan.

After the O.K. Corral shoot-out, Josie and Wyatt, on the run from the law, traveled throughout the West. For a while, they lived with Josie's parents in San Francisco. They owned mines and real estate and operated saloons and gambling parlors. Finally, they settled in southern California and started work on Wyatt's autobiography about his life as a marshal. When Wyatt Earp died, Josie buried his ashes in her family's plot at the Little Hills of Eternity, a Jewish cemetery in Colma, California. When she died, she was buried next to him.

A GREAT ADVENTURE

Other Jewish settlers had much less dramatic lives as they headed across the great American West. Although their numbers were small, as the country expanded westward, so did the Jewish community. And those Jewish settlers made important contributions to America.

Why was it important to the future of the Jewish community in America that Jewish pioneers helped settle the West?

Watch the movie about Wyatt Earp, Doc Holliday, and the Clanton gang, *Gunfight at the O.K. Corral.*

Read about the ḥalutzim, the "pioneers" who helped settle Palestine. How did their lives compare to those of the Jewish pioneers in America?

Immigrant brothers Adolph and Sam Frankel entered the United States through Galveston, Texas, and eventually owned clothing stores in Oklahoma and Texas.

Another gunfight

LOOK AT IT

Can you imagine a gunfight between a rabbi and the president of a synagogue over which prayer book to use? Rabbi Moses May and Abraham Waldman of Beth Israel in Portland, Oregon, had such a confrontation. The congregation was founded in 1859 and had a series of religious leaders before May had arrived. Services were conducted in the Orthodox tradition, using the prayer book *Minhag Ashkenaz*. May wanted to use *Minhag America*, published by Isaac Mayer Wise, and members of the congregation were divided between using *Minhag Ashkenaz* and *Minhag Portland* created by the board of directors of the synagogue.

Waldman, the president-elect of the synagogue, did not want to see the prayer book changed. He and the rabbi had been arguing for years, and their dispute erupted in a fistfight and shoot-out on a Friday morning in October 1880, under the window of the Esmond Hotel, where President Rutherford B. Hayes was staying. Rabbi May had been talking to a friend outside the hotel when Waldman came up behind him. Waldman grabbed May by the collar and hit him in the eyes, breaking his glasses. The rabbi pulled out a pistol and shot at his attacker. His first shot missed, but his second shot tore through Waldman's coat. Another man grabbed the rabbi before he could reload and shoot again.

The fight was covered in several newspapers. The *Daily Standard* of Portland headlined the story: "Pastoral Relations: How Rabbi May and Brother Waldman Serve The Lord." It ended by noting that "Waldman . . . a well known and highly respected citizen . . . was arrested in the afternoon . . . and fined for assault, but, as far as can be learned, Rabbi May was not molested." When the story was heard back east, Rabbi Isaac M. Wise wrote, "Mr. Waldman was not hurt, but the rabbi was soundly thrashed for being such a poor marksman." Wise ended by writing, "It is a pity that Israel should have produced a shooting clergyman."

from I. Harold Sharfman, *The First Rabbi: Origins of Conflict Between Orthodox and Reform: Jewish Polemic Warfare in pre–Civil War America: A Biographical History.* (Malibu, Calif.: J. Simon/Pangloss Press, 1988)

THINK ABOUT IT How would you feel about changes being made to your synagogue's prayer books? Who should decide on the changes? Who decides which special readings (prayers, songs, and poems), may be included in a prayer book in the first place? Are there prayers that should never be changed in any Jewish prayer book?

Sometimes, Jews in the west became cowboys. Here is one who was skilled in his chosen profession—Hominy's Famous Jewish Champion of the Lariat and Saddle.

CHAPTER 9

AMERICANIZING REFORM JUDAISM

What were some of the challenges that faced the American Jewish community of the mid–nineteenth century? How did the community react? How did these developments shape Jewish religious life in America?

By the middle of the nineteenth century, significant problems confronted the Jewish community in America. Many of the central European immigrants had chosen not to participate in synagogue life, and many had settled in frontier towns far from established Jewish communities. Fewer Jews kept kosher or educated their children Jewishly; many were more concerned with earning a living than with Jewish observance. They also wanted to be accepted by their Christian neighbors and become part of the secular American society. Protestant missionary groups tried to convert Jews to Christianity. And the everyday social interactions between Jews and non-Jews sometimes resulted in intermarriages. Thus, there were many reasons to make the changes that some American Jews believed would preserve Judaism while adapting it to American life.

IN THE BEGINNING

Even before the arrival of the central European Jewish immigrants, some Jews in America were ready for change. Others fought it, arguing that Jews must not tamper with traditional practices. During the 1820s, some young Jews in New York and Charleston had begun to embrace the Reform movement. It seemed appropriate, given the new democratic nature of the country. In New York, some Jews created Hebra Hinuch Nearim, an independent organization to educate Jewish youth. The group planned a worship service that was less formal than a traditional service. There was no formal leader, and time was set aside for explanations and instruction.

In 1824, a group of Jews in Charleston, led by Abraham Moise, Penina Moise's brother, and the editor and playwright Isaac Harby, asked the leaders of Congregation K. K. (Kehilat Kodesh) Beth Elohim to make certain changes in the Shabbat service. They wanted each Hebrew prayer to be followed by an English translation, new prayers relating to American life to be added to the service, a shorter service, and a sermon in English explaining the weekly Torah portion. Harby and his friends believed that these changes would make the service easier to understand and more appealing. Harby wrote, "We wish not to overthrow but to rebuild, not to destroy but to reform."

The leaders of the synagogue refused even to consider the request. So the members of Harby's group created the Reformed Society of Israelites for Promoting True Principles of Judaism According to Its Purity and Spirit. They found a place to meet, wrote their own prayer book, and used music in their services.

DO IT

Review the *halachah* for the observance of Shabbat. Remember, there are thirty-nine categories of activity that traditionally are not permitted on Shabbat. Write about which one of the thirty-nine categories is most difficult for you to observe and which one is the easiest.

Reform or reformed?

Reform refers to a continuing process of change and development. *Reformed* refers to a process that has been completed. In *Explaining Reform Judaism,* Eugene Borowitz and Naomi Patz point out that even though the first Reform congregation in America called itself Reformed; modern Reform Jews do not use the past tense to refer to their movement.

The leaders of Beth Elohim never stopped criticizing the reformers. Over time, the society's members grew discouraged, and its leaders died or drifted away. Harby moved to New York in 1827 and died in 1828. When he left Charleston, the small group of reformers who remained gave up its plan to build a new congregation and eventually drifted back to Beth Elohim. The reformers continued to work for acceptance of their ideas, however. The society never officially disbanded, but by the late 1830s it no longer existed.

A fire destroyed Beth Elohim in 1838. When the congregation met to plan for a new building, a group of reformers asked that an organ be installed. They were supported by the *ḥazan,* Gustavus Poznanski, even though playing an instrument on Shabbat was a violation of *halachah.* Poznanski had come to Charleston as a traditionalist but had come to favor reform. The congregation voted for the organ, and the more traditional members left to form a new Orthodox congregation, which they called Shearith Israel.

In your opinion, how should synagogue members make decisions about changes in the service?

Beth Elohim became the first "organ congregation" in America. Other innovations followed at Beth Elohim, such as confirmation classes for boys and girls and the elimination of the observance of the second day of holidays, an observance that the ancient rabbis had prescribed for Jews outside the land of Israel. The reformers also revised the traditional **creed** concerning the coming of a personal messiah and the resurrection of the dead in the messianic era. These beliefs were no longer meaningful to many Jews.

Some members and former members of the congregation so strongly opposed these changes, that they went to court to try to gain control of the synagogue. After three years, the courts ruled that religious choices were not an issue for the courts and should be decided by majority rule.

The controversy over the organ separated the reformers from the more traditional Jews, who began to call themselves Orthodox. According to the rabbi of the new Orthodox synagogue in Charleston, the term meant "true adherence to our holy religion in its ancient form."

A **creed** is a statement of belief.

RABBIS ARRIVE

Around this time, ordained rabbis began arriving in the United States from Europe. The first of these was Abraham Rice, who came to the Baltimore Hebrew Congregation from Bavaria in 1840. Strictly traditional, he never learned to speak English properly and rejected attempts to make him or his congregation more American.

Other rabbis, with both university degrees and formal rabbinic training, followed Rice. They worked to raise the level of Jewish religious practice and traditional scholarship in America. Now, **lay leaders,** after years of making the important decisions, found their power diminished. Many believed that they had built their synagogues and were not willing to allow the rabbis to make key decisions. By the 1850s and 1860s, urban congregations were large enough to be selective in their choice of a rabbi. Sometimes rabbis were fired, or members of a congregation moved to a congregation whose rabbi they liked better. Congregations in the bigger cities began to compete for members. The smaller communities continued to hire less skilled leaders.

Lay leaders are volunteer members of an organization; they are not hired professional leaders.

Some of the newly arrived rabbis brought **radical** ideas with them. The Reform movement had begun in Germany in the early 1800s in response to events both within and outside the Jewish community. In that period, Jews in some areas of Germany were given rights as citizens. In other areas, Jews continued to struggle for **emancipation,** which was not granted to all German Jews until the country's unification in 1871. Many German Jews were therefore under pressure to prove themselves worthy of emancipation—that is, to prove that they could be good citizens and part of the larger society. At the same time, many Jews did not understand Hebrew, and some were leaving the community through **assimilation** or conversion. German Jews were thus trying to live in two worlds, and they found that some of the beliefs and practices of traditional Judaism were no longer meaningful or were an obstacle to their full integration into German society. Some turned to Reform as a solution to their dilemma.

 Radical means "drastic" or "extreme."

Emancipation means "freedom from a controlling force."

Assimilation is the process of absorbing one group's culture into that of a dominant group.

The new central European immigrants in the United States strengthened the push for reform that had already begun in this country. Where Isaac Leeser had defended traditional ideas, several of the newly arrived rabbis rejected them. Leeser had minimized his own differences with Orthodoxy in order to promote unity among American Jews. Sometimes the new rabbis pushed for more changes, and sometimes the pressure for change came from their congregants. By 1855, Reform congregations had begun in Charleston, New York, Baltimore, Cincinnati, and Albany. The number of Reform congregations grew quickly, as did the size of the congregations. Over time, many of them became more radical in their practices.

Reform was able to become more radical in the United States than in Germany. Germany was more traditional, and America was more liberal and democratic. American reformers were committed to individual rights and to experimentation, whereas European reformers had to work within a united, traditional Jewish community.

The reformers introduced prayers in the **vernacular,** so that everyone could understand them. They also eliminated the repetition of prayers. Traditionally, prayers were said quietly by the congregation, then repeated in Hebrew by the *hazan* so that worshippers who did not know Hebrew could have the prayers said for them. But with services in English, the repetition no longer seemed necessary.

 The **vernacular** is the language of everyday, ordinary speech.

Removing certain prayers shortened the service. Over the years, many Hebrew poems, called *piyyutim,* had been added. Most worshippers in America had difficulty understanding them, however, so the reformers omitted them. Other prayers were eliminated because they spoke of the Jews' age-old hope of returning from exile to the land of Israel to rebuild the Temple in Jerusalem. Because these Jews believed they were now free and equal citizens of America, they thought that such prayers were inappropriate. At the dedication of the Reform congregation in Charleston in 1841, Gustavus Poznanski said, "This country is our Palestine, this city our Jerusalem, this house of God our Temple."

What did Gustavus Poznanski's statement mean?

Why was prayer in Hebrew considered important from a traditional viewpoint? Is it important today to pray in Hebrew? Why? Is it important to pray in English? Why? How do you feel when you pray in each language?

Compare the prayers

This prayer, written by Kaufmann Kohler, appeared in the first *Union Prayer Book*, published in 1895.

Grant us peace, thy most precious gift, O Thou eternal source of peace, and enable Israel to be a messenger of peace unto the peoples of the earth. Bless our country that it may ever be a stronghold of peace, and its advocate in the council of nations. May contentment reign within its borders, health and happiness within its homes. Strengthen the bonds of friendship and fellowship among all the inhabitants of our land. Plant virtue in every soul, and may the love of Thy name hallow every home and every heart. Praised be Thou, O Lord, Giver of Peace.

Here is the traditional version, translated from the Hebrew, as it was written at the time.

Grant peace, welfare, blessing, grace, lovingkindness, and mercy unto us and unto all Israel, thy people. Bless us O our Father, even all of us together, with the light of thy countenance; for by the light of thy countenance thou hast given us, O lord our God, the law of life, lovingkindness and righteousness, blessing, mercy, life and peace; and may it be good in thy sight to bless thy people Israel at all times and in every hour with thy peace. Blessed art thou, O lord, who blessest thy people Israel with peace.

Compare the two versions. What are the main differences? What is similar? Which of these versions speaks to you more powerfully? Write your comments below.

_____

_____

_____

_____

_____

_____

_____

_____

_____

In New York, Reform Jews founded Congregation Emanu-El in 1845. In addition to organ music, Emanu-El instituted hymns and sermons in German, the language that most of its congregants spoke, and a shorter service. Leo Merzbacher, the congregation's leader, composed America's first Reform prayer book written by a rabbi, *Seder Tefilah: The Order of Prayer for Divine Service,* which filled two volumes. This congregation became the choice of many of the city's richest and most successful Jews.

What is your reaction to the changes that Reform was making in traditional Judaism? What were the positive results of these changes? What were the negative results?

A MODERATE REFORM LEADER

As the Reform movement grew, its most important leader was Isaac Mayer Wise. Born in 1819 in Bohemia, Wise came to the United States in 1846. Even though he had received advanced training in Judaism and had taught for three years, he was unable to become a rabbi in Bohemia because he did not have a university education, a legal requirement. In America, he was offered the position of rabbi at Congregation Beth El in Albany.

Wise made a series of changes in the ritual of his new synagogue and organized a choir of men and women. He also spoke out in favor of Reform ideas, denying belief in a personal messiah and in the resurrection of the dead. After several disagreements on these and other matters, the president of the congregation, Louis Spanier, fired Wise just two days before Rosh Hashanah. Nonetheless, Wise occupied the synagogue's pulpit on Rosh Hashanah, an act that led to a physical confrontation between the two men and a general riot that was broken up by the sheriff. On the second day of Rosh Hashanah, Wise conducted services in his own home.

Some loyal followers organized a new congregation for Wise to lead, called Anshe Emet, ("Men of Truth"). Wise called himself an Orthodox reformer, someone who favored of "moderate reforms but not . . . violent transitions." And he introduced some moderate reforms at Anshe Emet, including the use of an organ and choir at Shabbat services, the elimination of prayers calling for the restoration of sacrifices, and the seating of men and women together.

In 1854, Wise went to Congregation Bene Yeshurun in Cincinnati, where he was promised a position for life. At that time, he had no intention of leading a revolution; he intended to make changes within traditional Judaism. He wanted to do away with practices that seemed "old-fashioned" or "impractical" and thought that all American Jews would accept his kind of modern Reform Judaism. Therefore, he called the prayer book he published *Minhag America,* hoping it would unite American Jews around a common prayer service.

Wise edited a weekly English-language newspaper called *The American Israelite* (originally *Israelite*) and another, in German, which was mainly for women, called *The Deborah.* He loved American life and culture and worked hard to share his enthusiasm with other American Jews. He was especially moved by debates he witnessed in the gallery of the U.S. Senate. Wise believed that Jewish immigrants needed to be as American as possible and saw Reform as a way of achieving that. In *The American Israelite,* he wrote, "As citizens we must not be distinct from the rest. In religion only are we Jews, and in all other respects we are American citizens." He traveled throughout the Midwest and South, dedicating several Reform synagogues. Many American Jews used his *siddur* and were influenced by his views.

Do you agree with Wise? What conflicts have you experienced between being a practicing, identified Jew and being an American?

One year after arriving in Cincinnati, Wise invited American Jewish leaders to gather in Cleveland. His goal was to unify American Jews and establish a rabbinical school in the United States. Isaac Leeser attended Wise's conference, but most traditional rabbis did not.

In 1873, Wise tried again, this time with the support of rabbis from other Reform synagogues in the Midwest. At that meeting, participants established the Union of

Rabbi Wise Reports

Wise's hopes for a unified American Judaism were reflected in his reports, written as he visited congregations in Indiana and Illinois.

1857. Lafayette [Indiana] is quite a place. . . . The Israelites of this and a neighboring place, Delphi, about thirty families in all, are united in a congregation, have a chazzen . . . a temporary synagogue, a burial ground, and are now about establishing a school. They live quite neighborly together, but in congregational matters they cannot boast much progress. They should have a better synagogue . . . and should be less divided in opinion in regard to school and other congregational matters. . . .

1856. Here I sit in Chicago, a miniature New York. . . . In regard to benevolence and charity the Chicago Israelites are by no means behind their brethren anywhere. The Hebrew Benevolent Societies and the Ladies Benevolent Societies are as flourishing and well supported here as in all the larger congregations of our country. . . . The Hebrew School . . . is a flourishing and well attended school. This school is supported by the congregation and every child, rich and poor, finds an excellent opportunity to receive a thorough English education and instruction in Hebrew, Bible, etc., and also in the German language.

I have to mention but one unpleasant fact. The congregation stands divided in a German and Polish congregation. . . . This is an unhappy situation . . . Why should American Jews not be united in all respects? "Have we not all one father, has not one God created us?"

from Kenneth Libo and Irving Howe, *We Lived There Too: In Their Own Words and Pictures—Pioneer Jews and the Westward Movement, 1630–1930* **(New York: St. Martin's/Marek, 1984)**

American Hebrew Congregations (UAHC), an organization of Reform congregations, and made a commitment to set up a rabbinical school. Hebrew Union College (HUC) was begun in Cincinnati in 1875 with Wise as president, and the first rabbis graduated in 1883.

The "Treifah Banquet"

LOOK AT IT

Menu of the "Treifah Banquet"

This is part of the menu, as reported in *The Cincinnati Enquirer* on July 12, 1883:

Little Neck Clams (half shell)
Potages (soup)
Poissons (fish)
Fillet de Boef, aux Champignons
(beef with mushrooms)
Soft-Shell Crabs
Salade de Shrimps (shrimp salad)
Sweet Breads a la Monglas
Petits Pois (peas) a la Francais
Poulets (chicken) a la Viennoise,
Asperges Sauce
Vinaigrette Pommes Pate (potato pie)
Grenouiles (frogs' legs) a la
Creme
Vol aux Vents de
Pigeons a la
Tryolienne
Sucres
(candies)
Ice Cream
Assorted and
Ornamented
Cakes

Find the laws of kashrut in Leviticus 11 and Deuteronomy 14:4-21. List the foods on the banquet menu that are treif.

A banquet was held at The Highland House, a famous and fancy resort in Cincinnati, to celebrate the graduation of the first class of rabbis from the Hebrew Union College. The meal was supposed to be kosher so as not to offend the more traditional guests. However, the first course was clams, and several people immediately walked out! A look at the menu shows that almost every course included food that violated kashrut. Some historians say that this happened by mistake; others say that it was done on purpose to show that the laws of kashrut were no longer relevant or important.

LEARN IT

Treif food is not kosher and is forbidden by *halachah*.

Kashrut refers to the Jewish dietary laws.

THINK ABOUT IT

What is your opinion about what happened at the "Treifah Banquet"?

from Elliot N. Dorff, *Conservative Judaism: Our Ancestors to Our Descendants.* (New York: United Synagogue of America, 1977)

Wise's position on change was not always clear, since he was more concerned with unifying the American Jewish community than with being consistent. While more traditional Jews thought Wise was too radical, he generally saw himself and his followers as moderates. He clearly favored Reform ideas, such as omitting some parts of the traditional service and observance of the second day of certain holidays. But like many leaders of the Reform movement in Germany, he wanted to keep most of the prayers in Hebrew.

CLICK ON IT

Visit the websites of the Hebrew Union College www.huc.edu and the Union of American Hebrew Congregations www.urj.org to find out more about their history and development. The organization is now known as the Union for Reform Judaism.

DO IT

Find out how Wise's views are similar to or different from the philosophy of Reform Judaism in America today. Visit a Reform synagogue and take a tour of the sanctuary. How does it express the views of Reform Judaism? How does it differ from a Conservative, Reconstructionist, or Orthodox sanctuary? Speak with the rabbi, and ask any questions you have about Reform Judaism. Learn about how the movement has developed in recent years.

A RADICAL REFORM LEADER

Another early Reform leader was Rabbi David Einhorn, who was born in Bavaria in 1808. He studied at a rabbinical seminary and then at a university and, by the time he graduated, had abandoned Orthodoxy for Reform. He came to the United States in 1855 to lead Har Sinai in Baltimore. Einhorn was concerned with social justice and supported greater participation in religious life by women and an end to slavery in the United States. His **abolitionist** position was not popular in Baltimore, and a pro-slavery mob forced him to flee the city. During the Civil War, he was the rabbi of Reform Congregation Keneseth Israel in Philadelphia. In 1866, Einhorn moved to New York.

 An **abolitionist** was in favor of doing away with—abolishing—slavery.

Einhorn's ideas were those of radical reform. He said that Judaism had reached a point where "all customs . . . as are lifeless must be abolished" in order to keep Jews within the community. Religious laws were being violated, and the daily prayers no longer expressed people's true feelings. These circumstances, he said, are "a **rent** in Judaism which threatens its very life and which no covering, however glittering, can repair." Unlike Wise, he saw no value in compromising for the sake of unity. The motto of radical Reform was "first truth, then peace." Einhorn saw the **Talmud** as valuable but believed that it misinterpreted biblical texts and introduced many insignificant religious regulations. Therefore, he was appalled by the resolution accepting talmudic authority that had been adopted at the meeting that Wise had held in Cleveland in 1855. Einhorn disliked any type of religious authority; freedom was his most prized value. He called Judaism "the religion of freedom."

 A **rent** is a tear.

The **Talmud** is the authoritative body of Jewish law and tradition comprising the Mishnah and the Gemara.

Even though Einhorn produced his own magazine, *Sinai,* and a Reform prayer book, *Olat Tamid,* he did not have the same effect on American Jews that Wise did. He was serious and scholarly, spoke mostly in German, and wrote long, dense articles. His ideas did have an important impact, however. He was a strong influence on his son-in-law, Kaufmann

A Story About An Organ

When Keneseth Israel's new building was dedicated in 1864, an organ was one of the building's most talked about, and controversial, features. It was the first synagogue in Philadelphia to have one. The story is told that Rabbi Einhorn met the rabbi of another synagogue on the street one day. Einhorn referred to the new building and the other rabbi burst out, "Ja, Einhorn, ich hors du hast ein orgle! Mit diesen orgle schneiden sie sich in den gorgle!" ("Yes, Einhorn, I hear you have an organ! With this organ you will cut your throat!")

from Shelley Kapnek Rosenberg, *Reform Congregation Keneseth Israel: 150 Years* (Philadelphia: Keneseth Israel, 1997)

Kohler, who called together the conference that wrote the Pittsburgh Platform, which set forth the main ideas of American Reform Judaism at that time.

THE PITTSBURGH PLATFORM

In 1885, nineteen Reform rabbis meeting in Pittsburgh passed a resolution stating that many of the beliefs and practices of traditional Judaism were no longer meaningful or relevant. Reform would continue to accept only the "moral laws" and those ceremonies that were "adapted to the views of modern civilization." The resolution also stated that Judaism was a religious community, not a nation, and that Jews, therefore, need not return to Palestine.

 The Reform movement has since changed its position on a return to Palestine (now Israel). How might the original position have affected your decision to join a Reform congregation?

Some reformers wanted to change the Sabbath service from Saturday to Sunday. They saw this change as an answer to the lack of interest that many Jews seemed to have in attending services. Rabbi Joseph Krauskopf, a graduate of

The Pittsburgh Platform

The Pittsburgh Platform said, among other things,

Today we accept as binding only its moral laws, and maintain only such ceremonies as elevate and sanctify our lives, but reject all such as are not adapted to the views and habits of modern civilization.

We hold that all such Mosaic and rabbinical laws as regulate diet, priestly purity, and dress, originated in ages and under the influence of ideas entirely foreign to our present mental and spiritual state . . . [and are] apt rather to obstruct than to further modern spiritual elevation. . . . We consider ourselves no longer a nation, but a religious community, and therefore expect neither a return to Palestine . . . nor the restoration of any of the laws concerning the Jewish state.

List the main beliefs of the Reform movement as expressed in this section of the Pittsburgh Platform. Read about the movement today, and list other beliefs that are central to Reform Judaism. What has changed? What remains the same?

Prepare to debate the question of whether Judaism is a religion or a nation.

the Hebrew Union College, said, "The present Saturday farce is a disgrace and works greater havoc in our ranks than ever a Sunday observance could possibly do." Some rabbis persuaded their congregations to go along with the idea. Rabbi Wise and a few of his colleagues thought it would be better to hold the Friday-evening service not at sunset when Shabbat begins, but later in the evening. Late-Friday-evening services soon became the general practice in many Reform congregations. At its founding, in 1889, the Central Conference of American Rabbis (CCAR), an organization of Reform rabbis, adopted the Pittsburgh Platform. That document remained the major statement of the movement's positions until it was revised in the Columbus Platform in 1937.

What is your opinion of holding Sabbath services on Sunday?

TRADITION AND CHANGE

By 1860, there were twelve "organ congregations" in America; eight years later, there were thirty. By 1880, the majority of American Jews who belonged to synagogues considered themselves Reform. Changes had come quickly, even if radicals like David Einhorn thought they were too slow. Mixed seating—men and women sitting together—and the elimination of the second days of holiday observance became common. Some synagogues shortened Torah readings and recited more prayers in the vernacular.

However, the unity of Jews in America that Leeser and Wise had hoped for was not to be. The gap between traditional and Reform Jews continued to widen.

Why is it important to maintain certain Jewish traditions? Which practices should be changed? Why?

Nominate someone to the Jewish-American Hall of Fame. Go to www.amuseum.org/jahf. You might choose someone you have read about in this book—or someone else who you think has made a contribution to the American Jewish community.

Matching Game

Match the names in column A with the descriptions in column B.

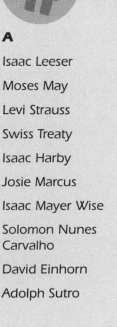

A	B
Isaac Leeser	"Christians alone are entitled"
Moses May	mayor
Levi Strauss	Frémont expedition
Swiss Treaty	UAHC and HUC
Isaac Harby	*Olat Tamid*
Josie Marcus	*Catechism for Younger Children*
Isaac Mayer Wise	501
Solomon Nunes Carvalho	Reformed Society of Israelites
David Einhorn	"shooting clergyman"
Adolph Sutro	Wyatt Earp

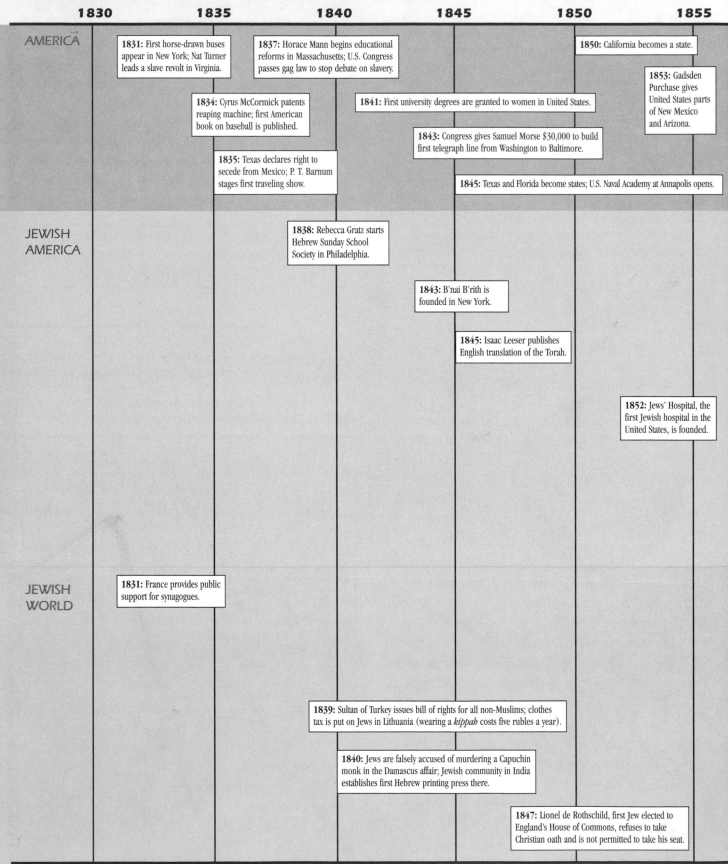

1830   **1835**   **1840**   **1845**   **1850**   **1855**

AMERICA

1831: First horse-drawn buses appear in New York; Nat Turner leads a slave revolt in Virginia.

1837: Horace Mann begins educational reforms in Massachusetts; U.S. Congress passes gag law to stop debate on slavery.

1850: California becomes a state.

1853: Gadsden Purchase gives United States parts of New Mexico and Arizona.

1834: Cyrus McCormick patents reaping machine; first American book on baseball is published.

1841: First university degrees are granted to women in United States.

1843: Congress gives Samuel Morse $30,000 to build first telegraph line from Washington to Baltimore.

1835: Texas declares right to secede from Mexico; P. T. Barnum stages first traveling show.

1845: Texas and Florida become states; U.S. Naval Academy at Annapolis opens.

JEWISH AMERICA

1838: Rebecca Gratz starts Hebrew Sunday School Society in Philadelphia.

1843: B'nai B'rith is founded in New York.

1845: Isaac Leeser publishes English translation of the Torah.

1852: Jews' Hospital, the first Jewish hospital in the United States, is founded.

JEWISH WORLD

1831: France provides public support for synagogues.

1839: Sultan of Turkey issues bill of rights for all non-Muslims; clothes tax is put on Jews in Lithuania (wearing a *kippah* costs five rubles a year).

1840: Jews are falsely accused of murdering a Capuchin monk in the Damascus affair; Jewish community in India establishes first Hebrew printing press there.

1847: Lionel de Rothschild, first Jew elected to England's House of Commons, refuses to take Christian oath and is not permitted to take his seat.

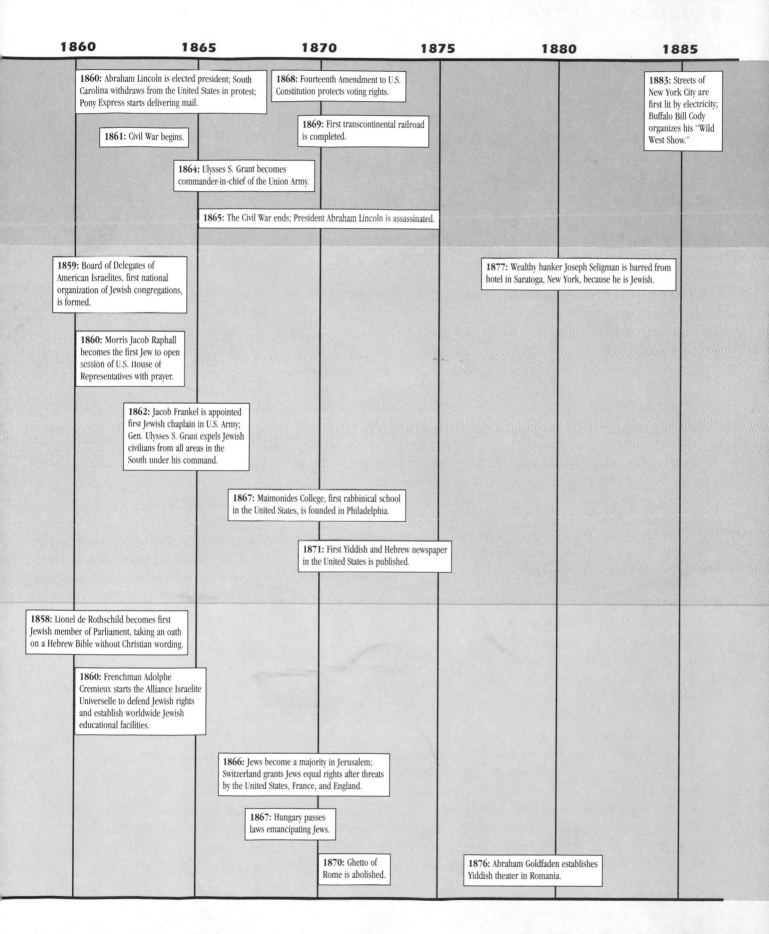

1860   **1865**   **1870**   **1875**   **1880**   **1885**

1860: Abraham Lincoln is elected president; South Carolina withdraws from the United States in protest; Pony Express starts delivering mail.

1868: Fourteenth Amendment to U.S. Constitution protects voting rights.

1883: Streets of New York City are first lit by electricity; Buffalo Bill Cody organizes his "Wild West Show."

1861: Civil War begins.

1869: First transcontinental railroad is completed.

1864: Ulysses S. Grant becomes commander-in-chief of the Union Army.

1865: The Civil War ends; President Abraham Lincoln is assassinated.

1859: Board of Delegates of American Israelites, first national organization of Jewish congregations, is formed.

1877: Wealthy banker Joseph Seligman is barred from hotel in Saratoga, New York, because he is Jewish.

1860: Morris Jacob Raphall becomes the first Jew to open session of U.S. House of Representatives with prayer.

1862: Jacob Frankel is appointed first Jewish chaplain in U.S. Army; Gen. Ulysses S. Grant expels Jewish civilians from all areas in the South under his command.

1867: Maimonides College, first rabbinical school in the United States, is founded in Philadelphia.

1871: First Yiddish and Hebrew newspaper in the United States is published.

1858: Lionel de Rothschild becomes first Jewish member of Parliament, taking an oath on a Hebrew Bible without Christian wording.

1860: Frenchman Adolphe Cremieux starts the Alliance Israelite Universelle to defend Jewish rights and establish worldwide Jewish educational facilities.

1866: Jews become a majority in Jerusalem; Switzerland grants Jews equal rights after threats by the United States, France, and England.

1867: Hungary passes laws emancipating Jews.

1870: Ghetto of Rome is abolished.

1876: Abraham Goldfaden establishes Yiddish theater in Romania.

THE CURRICULUM DEVELOPMENT TEAM

Shelley Kapnek Rosenberg, Ed.D.

Dr. Shelley Kapnek Rosenberg is the author of *Raising a Mensch: How to Bring Up Ethical Children in Today's World*, (2003) and *Adoption and the Jewish Family: Contemporary Perspectives* (1998). Dr. Rosenberg earned her Ed.D. in psychoeducational processes from Temple University. Since 1994, she has worked for the Auerbach Central Agency for Jewish Education.

Alice L. George, Ph.D.

After twenty years as an editor at newspapers such as the *Detroit Free Press* and the *Philadelphia Daily News*, Alice L. George left journalism to earn a Ph.D. in history at Temple University, which she received in 2001. Her award-winning doctoral dissertation has been turned into a book, *Awaiting Armageddon: How Americans Faced the Cuban Missile Crisis* (2003).

Reena Sigman Friedman, Ph.D.

Dr. Reena Sigman Friedman is Associate Professor of Modern Jewish Civilization at the Reconstructionist Rabbinical College. She is the author of *These Are Our Children: Jewish Orphanages in the United States, 1880–1925* (1994) and numerous articles and publications. Dr. Friedman is also a faculty member of the Florence Melton Adult Mini-School.

Jonathan D. Sarna, Ph.D.

Jonathan D. Sarna is the Joseph H. and Belle R. Braun Professor of American Jewish History at Brandeis University. Dr. Sarna has written, edited, or co-edited twenty books. Articles, reviews, and commentaries by Dr. Sarna appear regularly in scholarly and popular journals, as well as in Jewish newspapers across North America. He is the author of *American Judaism: A History* (2004).

Nancy M. Messinger

Nancy Messinger has been the Director of Educational Resources at the Auerbach Central Agency for Jewish Education for the past thirteen years. She is also the website coordinator for www.acaje.org. Ms. Messinger earned a B.H.L. from the Jewish Theological Seminary, a certificate of Jewish librarianship from Gratz College, a B.S. in history from Columbia University, and an M.S. in counseling from Villanova University.

Rochelle Buller Rabeeya

Rochelle Rabeeya is the Director of Educational Services at the Auerbach Central Agency for Jewish Education. She holds an M.A. and an honorary doctorate in Jewish education from Hebrew Union College–Jewish Institute of Religion and has done post-graduate studies in educational psychology. At ACAJE, she focuses on training school committees, helping schools develop a systemic approach to Jewish education, developing curriculums and coordinating staff development.

Helene Z. Tigay

Helene Z. Tigay has been the Executive Director of the Auerbach Central Agency for Jewish Education since 1990. She has a B.S. in psychology from Columbia University, a B.R.E. in Hebrew literature from the University of Pennsylvania, and has been in the doctoral program in psychological services at the University of Pennsylvania's Graduate School of Education. She has written articles on a variety of topics and is a recipient of the United Synagogue of Conservative Judaism's Ateret Kavod Award.

Julia Prymak

Julia Prymak is the owner of Pryme Design, a graphic design and production services company that manages all aspects of clients' print and promotional needs. She earned her B.F.A. from Rochester Institute of Technology.

Nancy Isserman

Nancy Isserman is the Director of the Challenge and Change: American Jewish History Curriculum Project, and the Associate Director of the Feinstein Center for American Jewish History at Temple University, where she has been since 1992. She is currently working on her dissertation on the determinants of political tolerance in Holocaust survivors at the Graduate Center, City University of New York. She holds an M.S.W. from the George Warren Brown School of Social Work at Washington University.

Murray Friedman, Ph.D.

Dr. Friedman has been the Director of the Feinstein Center for American Jewish History at Temple University since its inception in 1990. He is Director Emeritus of the Philadelphia Chapter of the American Jewish Committee, where he worked for forty-three years. He was vice chairman of the U.S. Commission on Civil Rights from 1986–1989. Dr. Friedman received his Ph.D. from Georgetown University, in American political and social history. He has written numerous articles and books on American Jewish history.